T0406657

Just Transitions

Series Editor

Raphael J. Heffron, University of Pau and Pays de l'Adour, Pau, France

Victoria R. Nalule · Raphael J. Heffron ·
Damilola S. Olawuyi

Renegotiating Contracts for the Energy Transition in the Extractives Industry

palgrave
macmillan

Victoria R. Nalule
School of Law
University of Bradford
Bradford, UK

Raphael J. Heffron
University of Pau and Pays de l'Adour
Pau, France

Damilola S. Olawuyi
School of Law
Hamad bin Khalifa University
Doha, Qatar

ISSN 2731-6041 ISSN 2731-605X (electronic)
Just Transitions
ISBN 978-3-031-46257-3 ISBN 978-3-031-46258-0 (eBook)
https://doi.org/10.1007/978-3-031-46258-0

This Palgrave Macmillan imprint is published by the registered company Springer Nature Switzerland AG
The registered company address is: Gewerbestrasse 11, 6330 Cham, Switzerland

Paper in this product is recyclable.

Foreword by N. J. Ayuk

It is my pleasure to write a foreword for this valuable monograph by Dr. Victoria R. Nalule, Professor Raphael J. Heffron, and Professor Damilola S. Olawuyi.

Their book presents practical ways of renegotiating oil, natural gas, and coal project contracts in an era when countries are transitioning from fossil fuels to renewable energy sources.

The authors also look at risks associated with fossil fuel production today—including legal, financial, environmental, social, and political ones. They illustrate how the energy industry is evolving, with case studies that showcase countries around the globe and the measures they have adopted to help minimize the adverse effects of climate change.

Even as countries begin transitioning to renewables, however, fossil fuel exploration, production, distribution, and domestic usage remain vital in regions around the globe, including Africa. For developing nations, oil, gas, and coal remain key to ensuring energy security, growing and diversifying economies, and industrializing. Their leaders and energy industry stakeholders are tasked with doing everything possible to create a healthy energy mix—one that includes fossil fuels as well as renewable energy sources like wind, solar, and hydrogen power.

Contract negotiations, and re-negotiations, will be a key part of those efforts. The challenge will be finding common ground that allows companies to continue realizing a return on their investments while supporting climate goals—and continuing to meet the needs of host countries. It's quite a balancing act, considering the risks and billion-dollar commitments that international oil companies face while discussing practical measures these companies can take to minimize greenhouse gas emissions, including carbon capture, utilization, and storage (CCUS); participation in voluntary carbon markets; and avoiding routine natural gas flaring.

I always encourage those who will be participating in negotiations to prepare extensively. Their success depends on it. That's why this book, with practical advice, relevant industry information, and insights into the risks associated with exploration and production, is a valuable resource.

The three contributing authors have brought first-hand experiences from different countries. The book is timely, and it will be a great asset to professionals, government institutions, universities, and a wide range of natural resources stakeholders who are interested in understanding the energy transition and contract negotiations.

South Africa
September 2023

N. J. Ayuk
Executive Chairman
African Energy Chamber

Foreword by Ernest Rubondo

I am delighted to write a foreword for this important monograph put together by three distinguished professionals namely Dr. Victoria R. Nalule, who is very enthusiastic about global developments in the energy and extractive sector, together with her co-authors Professor Raphael J. Heffron and Professor Damilola S. Olawuyi.

The book brings out the dilemma of addressing climate change and ensuring energy security, which the world is currently grappling with, and also describes the policy actions being taken by countries in relation to the energy transition. It addresses in a unique way, the different risks associated with developing extractive projects in the energy transition era and delves into the legal, financial, environmental, social, and political risks associated with the extractives in different countries.

The book presents a succinct description of the ongoing global transition to clean and low-carbon energy sources and the resulting fundamental changes in the levels and modes of production, distribution, and commercialization of extractive resources worldwide. As countries, businesses, and other stakeholders adopt policies and targets aimed at constraining investments and actions that are believed to contribute to climate change, risk in the energy sector is on the rise. These issues are well elaborated in the book, with reference to case studies of various countries across the globe.

The impact the energy transition has, and continues to have on extractive contracts, together with potential reviews of existing extractive contractual provisions to meet the global net zero goals are well presented in the book. Analyses of various extractive contract provisions together with practical tools and strategies to address energy transition risks in the extractive industries are also presented.

The book concludes by recognizing the role the extractive sector is expected to play both in ensuring the supply of the energy transition minerals required for the energy transition, as well as in advancing a just, inclusive, and orderly transition.

This publication which presents first-hand experiences from different countries is timely and is going to be an important asset to academia, energy professionals, government institutions, extractive companies, and the different natural resources stakeholders interested in understanding energy transitions and extractive contract negotiations.

A very informative and enjoyable read.

October 2023

Ernest Rubondo
Executive Director
Petroleum Authority of Uganda
(PAU)
Kampala, Uganda

Preface

The world is transitioning to a low-carbon economy. This is crucial in order to address the climate change challenges that societies are experiencing globally. Indeed, tackling climate change is one of the recognized goals stipulated in the United Nations Sustainable Development Goal 13 (UN SDG). For this to happen there is a need to reduce reliance on extractive resources such as oil, gas, and coal so as to reduce the associated greenhouse gas emissions. In this context, the geographies of energy transitions have to be taken into consideration. In essence, this implies that different countries face different energy challenges. For instance, in recent years, different countries that had made progress in transitioning to clean energy have been forced to re-invest in fossil fuels as a way of addressing energy security in their countries. Other countries such as those in the Global South are still relying on fossil fuels to achieve the UN SDG 7 on energy access. The global energy crisis experienced in 2021 also made some countries question the practicability of saying goodbye to fossil fuels. Specifically, the geopolitics in Europe (Russia-Ukraine war) and coupled with ineffective energy policies, partly contributed to the global energy crisis. Ideally, with the energy transitions, countries should be able to shift from traditional energy to modern energy; from fossil fuels to clean energy sources.

The ongoing global transition to clean and low-carbon energy sources, therefore, is resulting in fundamental changes in the levels and modes of production, distribution, and commercialization of extractive resources worldwide. As countries, businesses, and other stakeholders adopt policies and targets aimed at constraining investments and actions that contribute to the adverse effects of climate change, risk in the energy sector is also on the rise. These include financial risks, governance risks, and social risks. Such risks affect different stakeholders including host governments, energy investors, and communities. Consequently, the increasing uncertainties exacerbate governance risks making it harder for countries to meet their net zero targets due to the need to invest in more oil and gas to address the energy security issues. The twenty-first-century dilemma, therefore, relates to how we can address climate change and at the same time tackle energy security challenges. Therefore, existing and new contractual arrangements in the extractive sector more broadly will need to respond to the challenges of the energy transition risks identified above. This book, therefore, reviews the existing extractive contractual provisions and suggests how these can be renegotiated to meet the global net zero goals.

This book will be a first in the energy law literature to focus on renegotiating extractive contracts to align with the net-zero goals. It delves into extractive contract negotiations in four ways which collectively represent a major research gap in the literature. It will focus on extractive contract provisions (a) in detail, (b) in a theoretical way, (c) examine their alignment with net zero goals, and (d) suggest how these provisions could be renegotiated to ensure effective energy transition. Consequently, the book will assess how contractual provisions are responding to, or reflecting energy transition scenarios, and highlight areas to be included or strengthened to minimize transitions-related risks for all energy stakeholders.

Bradford, UK — Victoria R. Nalule
Pau, France — Raphael J. Heffron
Doha, Qatar — Damilola S. Olawuyi

Acknowledgments

Victoria R. Nalule
I sincerely thank Nalule Energy and Minerals Consultants (NEM Energy) for their support and research idea. Their work in the different parts of the globe has been influential in this research.

Raphael J. Heffron
I would like to thank all who contributed in some form to the development of this short book.

I also convey thanks to people I have worked with over the years from across the world and who I have learnt more on how the energy sector works and the justice issues that arise in the USA, Europe, Asia-Pacific, Africa, Middle East, North, and Latin America.

Le haghaidh mo h-oileán

Damilola S. Olawuyi
Umair Dogar (Qatar Foundation) deserves special appreciation for providing remarkable and thoughtful research assistance.

Contents

About the Authors

Dr. Victoria R. Nalule is a Lawyer and a renowned expert in Climate Change, Energy, and Mining Law. She has extensive experience working on various projects in the different parts of the Globe. She is a holder of a Ph.D. in International Energy Law and Policy (Dundee, UK). She is the CEO of Nalule Energy and Minerals Consultants (NEM Energy). She is also currently lecturing Energy and Mining law at the University of Bradford, in the United Kingdom.

She has a growing international track record in the energy and mining sectors. She has authored eight books in the energy and mining sectors with reputable publishers; and various journal articles.

She is enthusiastic about energy arbitration & dispute resolution. As such, she is an Arbitrator at the Energy Disputes Arbitration Center (EDAC), Turkey. She is a committee member at the International Law Association (ILA). She offers extensive experience in Climate Change, the Energy and Mining sectors having worked with various institutions; regional and international organizations including assignments for the Extractive Industries Transparency Initiative (EITI); The African Union through the African Mining Atlas; The Queen Mary University of London (EU Energy Project); The International Energy Charter Secretariat in Belgium; to mention but a few.

Professor Raphael J. Heffron is Professor in Energy Law, Justice, the Social Contract, and Sustainability at the Universite de Pau et des

Pays de l'Adour, Pau, France. He is also ***Jean Monnet Professor in the Just Transition to a Low-Carbon Economy*** awarded by the European Commission (2019–2022). In 2020, he was appointed as ***Senior Counsel at Janson*** law firm in Brussels (Belgium). He is a qualified Barrister-at-Law, and a graduate of both Oxford (M.Sc.-Christ Church) and Cambridge (M.Phil.-Darwin & Ph.D.-Trinity Hall). He also holds degrees from the University of St. Andrews (M.Litt.), and Trinity College Dublin (B.A., M.A.).

His work all has a principal focus on achieving a sustainable and just transition to a low-carbon economy, and combines a mix of law, policy, and economics. He has published over 190 publications of different types and is the most cited scholar in his field worldwide for energy law, energy justice, and just transition worldwide (3400+ *Scopus/6500+ Googlescholar*) with translated work in multiple languages including Chinese, Italian, French, Spanish, Portuguese, Arabic, and Persian. He has given just over 200 keynotes or guest lectures in 63 countries worldwide.

Professor Damilola S. Olawuyi is a Professor and UNESCO Chair on Environmental Law and Sustainable Development at the Hamad Bin Khalifa University (HBKU) College of Law, Doha, Qatar. He is also the Director of the Institute for Oil, Gas, Energy, Environment, and Sustainable Development at the Afe Babalola University, Nigeria. He holds a doctorate in energy and environmental law from the University of Oxford; a Master of Laws (LL.M.) from Harvard University; and another LL.M. from the University of Calgary. He is an Independent Expert on the United Nations Working Group on Business and Human Rights; Vice Chair of the International Law Association; and Chair of the Association of Environmental Law Lecturers in Middle East and North African Universities (ASSELLMU). He was formerly an Independent Expert on the African Union's Working Group on extractive industries, environment, and human rights violations in Africa.

He has published several articles, books, and reports on energy, environment, and natural resources law, including *Environmental Law in Arab States* (Oxford University Press, 2022), which received *the 2023 American Society of International Law (ASIL) Certificate of Merit for High Technical Craftsmanship and Utility to Practicing Lawyers.*

He provides legal advice and services on all aspects of energy, environment, and extractives law as a Senior Counsel at McNair International.

Abbreviations

AfCFTA	African Continental Free Trade Area
CONMESA	Common Market for Eastern and Southern Africa
COP	Conference of the Parties
DRC	Democratic Republic of Congo
DSM	Dispute Settlement Mechanism
EC	Extractive Company
EEZ	Exclusive Economic Zones
EI	Extractive Industries
EIA	Environmental Impact Assessment
EITI	Extractive Industries Transparency Initiative
ESG	Environmental, Social, and Governance
ET	Emission Trading
EU	European Union
EV	Electric Vehicle
FDI	Foreign Direct Investment
FPIC	Free, Prior, and Informed Consent
GDP	Gross Domestic Product
GDPG	Gross Domestic Product Growth
GHG	Greenhouse Gases
HC	Host Country
HDI	Human Development Index
ICCPR	International Covenant on Civil and Political Rights
IOC	International Oil Company
JOA	Joint Operating Agreement
LC	Local Content
LCRs	Local Content Requirements

MSG	Multistakeholder Group
NDC	Nationally Determined Contribution
PSA	Petroleum Sharing Agreement
SSA	Sub-Saharan Africa

List of Tables

CHAPTER 1

The Energy Transition Global Landscape

Abstract Decarbonising the energy sector and all the various sectors of the economy has become a priority for many countries. This is in response to the need to address climate change, as stipulated in the 2015 Paris Agreement and the United Nations Sustainable Development Goal (UN SDG)13, which is focused on climate action. Specifically, this transformation is visible with the introduction of new low carbon technologies, which have to some extent been making it possible to embrace the energy transition. Although there is no agreed definition of what energy transition means, it is generally understood as a shift from fossil fuels to clean energy sources. This chapter therefore examines the global energy transition landscape. It spotlights the practical dilemma of addressing climate change and energy security.

Keywords Energy transition · Climate change · Energy access · Energy progression · Energy justice · Extractives · Net zero

Decarbonising the energy sector and all the various sectors of the economy has become a priority for many countries. This is in response to the need to address climate change, as stipulated in the 2015 Paris Agreement and the United Nations Sustainable Development Goal (UN

V. R. Nalule et al., *Renegotiating Contracts for the Energy Transition in the Extractives Industry*, Just Transitions,
https://doi.org/10.1007/978-3-031-46258-0_1

SDG)13, which is focused on climate action.[1] Specifically, this transformation is visible with the introduction of new low carbon technologies, which have to some extent been making it possible to embrace the energy transition.

Although there is no agreed definition of what energy transition means, it is generally understood as a shift from fossil fuels to clean energy sources. International organisations have endeavoured to define the term. For instance, the International Renewable Energy Agency (IRENA), defines energy transition as a pathway towards the transformation of the global energy sector from fossil-based to zero-carbon by the second half of this century.[2] According to IRENA, the focus of this transition is to tackle climate change by reducing energy-related CO_2 emissions and thereby increasing renewable energy and energy efficiency measures while at the same time reducing the consumption of fossil fuels.[3] Taking cognisance of the challenges of having a wholesome energy transition, experts have gone ahead to advocate for 'Energy Progression', which ensures the progressive use of energy resources while transitioning to a low carbon economy.[4]

Reducing or stopping the burning of fossil fuels has been spotlighted as the central solution to addressing climate change. Indeed, reliable data shows that fossil fuels are responsible for at least 75% of the global greenhouse gases, and nearly 90% of all carbon dioxide emissions.[5] The 2023 IPCC report spotlighted the need for immediate and deep emissions reductions across all the sectors. This would consequently require

[1] United Nations Sustainable Development Goals, https://sdgs.un.org/goals. Last accessed on 1 August 2023.

[2] International Renewable Energy Agency. 2018. Energy Transition. https://www.irena.org/energytransition. Last accessed on 1 August 2023.

[3] Ibid.

[4] Nalule, V.R., 'How to Respond to Energy Transitions in Africa: Introducing the Energy Progression Dialogue' (2021) *Energy Transitions and the Future of the African Energy Sector: Law, Policy and Governance*, 3–5.

[5] United Nations: Climate Action, https://www.un.org/en/climatechange/science/causes-effects-climate-change#:~:text=Fossil%20fuels%20%E2%80%93%20coal%2C%20oil%20and,of%20all%20carbon%20dioxide%20emissions. Last accessed on 1 June 2023.

reducing emissions by 43% by 2030, 60% by 2035 and reach net-zero in early 2050.[6]

In recent years, however, it has become evident that countries both in the global north and global south, are not ready for the energy transition in its entirety. In 2018, the UN Intergovernmental Panel on Climate Change (IPCC) issued a warning that humanity had just twelve years to limit global warming to below 2 °C. With the 2023 energy developments, we are left with just seven years to abide with the IPCC warning. Yet, there is no clear and effective strategy of how the energy transition could practically play out in different countries. The current IPCC 2023 report indeed emphasises that without immediate concerted action, it is no longer possible to limit the global rise to 1.5 °C this century. According to this report, the last decade was the warmest in the previous 125,000 years: and this global warming is caused by the greenhouse gases primarily produced by using fossil fuels.[7] This therefore is evidence that we urgently need to transition to a low carbon economy; and it should be noted that this transition should be 'just' and more will be stated on that later.[8]

1.1 Policy Actions Across Countries

Whereas some countries such Albania, Iceland and Paraguay have successfully been able to obtain 100% electrification from renewable energy. Other countries are still taking major initiatives to achieve this. For instance, the 2019 Dutch Climate Act sets ambitious targets to reduce greenhouse gas emissions by 49% by 2030 and by 95% by 2050 (compared to 1990 levels) and for 100% of electricity to come from

[6] IPCC, 2023: Summary for Policymakers. In: *Climate Change 2023: Synthesis Report. Contribution of Working Groups I, II and III to the Sixth Assessment Report of the Intergovernmental Panel on Climate Change* [Core Writing Team, H. Lee and J. Romero (eds.)]. IPCC, Geneva, Switzerland, pp. 1–34, https://doi.org/10.59327/IPCC/AR6-9789291691647.001.

[7] IPCC, 2023: Summary for Policymakers. In: *Climate Change 2023: Synthesis Report. Contribution of Working Groups I, II and III to the Sixth Assessment Report of the Intergovernmental Panel on Climate Change* [Core Writing Team, H. Lee and J. Romero (eds.)]. IPCC, Geneva, Switzerland, pp. 1–34, https://doi.org/10.59327/IPCC/AR6-9789291691647.001.

[8] Heffron, R.J., *Achieving a Just Transition to a Low-Carbon Economy* (Heidelberg, Germany: Springer, 2021).

renewables by 2050.[9] Despite these initiatives in various countries, in recent years, other countries such as the United Kingdom have made strong commitments to the continued investments in fossil fuels. For instance, on the 31st of July, 2023, the United Kingdom (UK) announced plans to allow a big expansion of drilling for oil and gas in the North Sea. The Prime Minister, Rishi Sunak was hopeful that, the plans would provide the UK with domestically sourced energy while it transitions to a net zero economy by 2050.[10] The Prime Minister further emphasised that the UK needs more oil and gas for their economy.[11]

In the United States of America, while coming into power, President Joe Biden had announced his support for 100% renewable energy. However, with the global energy crisis, the same president was eager to encourage the pumping of more fossil fuels from OPEC member countries. This was intended to address energy security issues and ensure that the population in the USA has access to affordable fuels. Data shows that the USA has produced more oil than any other country, and it currently has 40 billion barrels of reserves it intends to keep utilising. Indeed, the role of crude oil cannot be understated, as it is the worlds' main source of fuel. In 2020, the world used approximately 88.6 million barrels per day of oil, which amounted to 30.1% of the world's primary energy.

The UK and the USA are developed countries whose economic, social, pollical and energy challenges differ from those of the developed countries: hence necessitating for tailored solution to address the energy trilemma. Additionally, we also recall that once a hub for fossil fuels and having attained economic development from the oil and gas revenues, Norway has also taken strategic measures to embrace the energy transition. In June 2020, the Norwegian parliament recommended that the Sovereign wealth fund sells off more than $10 billion of stocks in companies related to fossil fuels.[12] This, in practice, implies that the country

[9] Climate Law (No. 253 of 2019).

[10] CNN BUSINESS NEWS, https://edition.cnn.com/2023/07/31/energy/sunak-north-sea-oil-gas-licenses/index.html. Last accessed on 1 August 2023.

[11] CNN BUSINESS NEWS, https://edition.cnn.com/2023/07/31/energy/sunak-north-sea-oil-gas-licenses/index.html. Last accessed on August 2023.

[12] Forbes: Norway Wealth Fund to Dumb Fossil Fuels Stock. 12 June 2020. Can be accessed at, https://www.forbes.com/sites/davidnikel/2019/06/12/norway-wealth-fund-to-dumpfossil-fuel-stocks-worth-billions-in-environmental-move/#4dbb5c9748a3. Last accessed 29 August 2023.

is shifting from fossil fuels to clean energy. In this respect, the Wealth Fund can no longer invest in companies that mine more than 20 million tonnes of coal annually or generate more than 10,000 MW of power using coal.[13]

Further, in November 2019, The European Investment Bank (EIB), approved a policy to ban funding for oil, gas and coal projects at the end of 2021. Since 2013, the EIB has funded a €13.4 billion of fossil fuel projects, and in 2018 alone, it funded about €2 billion worth of projects. With the ban, however, no more fossil fuel projects will be funded after 2021, although gas projects could still be funded as long as they are utilising clean technologies such as carbon capture and storage, combining heat and power generation, or mixing in renewable gases with the fossil natural gas.[14] Besides the reduction in fossil fuel funding, climate activists have also put massive pressure on investors.[15] For instance, in June 2019, Kenya halted the Lamu coal power project due to environmental concerns.[16] Protests against coal projects have also been evidenced in European countries such as Germany.[17]

While the above developments geared towards transitioning to a low carbon economy are visible, the reliance on fossil fuels is evident in different countries. With a lack of consensus on the global level on how to manage the energy transition, it becomes imperative to devise ways of how countries and relevant stakeholders can renegotiate contracts for the energy transition in the extractive industry. This is the focus of this book.

[13] Ibid. not used anymore.

[14] BBC News: European Investment Bank Drops Fossil Fuel Funding. 14 November 2019. Can be accessed at, https://www.bbc.co.uk/news/business-50427873. Last accessed 29 August 2023.

[15] Nalule, V.R., 'How to Respond to Energy Transitions in Africa: Introducing the Energy Progression Dialogue' (2021) *Energy Transitions and the Future of the African Energy Sector: Law, Policy and Governance*, 3–5.

[16] BBC News: Kenya halts Lamu Coal Power Project. 26 June 2019. Can be accessed at, https://www.bbc.co.uk/news/world-africa-48771519. Last accessed 29 August 2023.

[17] BBC News: Climate Protesters Storm Garzweiler Coalmine in Germany. 23 June 2019. Can be accessed at, https://www.bbc.co.uk/news/world-europe-48734321. Last accessed 29 August 2023.

1.2 The Geographies of Energy Transition

Whereas there are global efforts to address climate change by reducing the reliance on fossil fuels, we must recognise the geographies of the energy transition. Basically, this relates to the fact that different countries face different energy challenges. Hence, their levels of transitioning to a low carbon economy do differ, as such each country should embrace tailored solutions. For instance, data shows that 3 billion people which is more than 40% of the world population, are still relying on polluting and unhealthy fuels for cooking.[18] The figures are particularly worrying in Africa as reports show that 600 million people do not have access to electricity, and around 900 million people lack access to clean cooking facilities.[19]

There have been initiatives to address energy access challenges in developing countries such as those in Africa, however, these have also proved ineffective. Such initiatives include among others Sustainable Energy for All (SE4ALL) initiative, Japan's power infrastructure support programme, the US Power Africa initiative, and the EnDev programme (Germany, the Netherlands, the United Kingdom, and others). There is however a need for strong coordination among these various initiatives to avoid unnecessary duplication and to be able to ensure a maximum degree of synergy.[20]

The continued energy access challenges have not only made it hard for developing countries to attain economic development but have also led to deaths in some countries. For instance, in Uganda, it was reported that more than one hundred fifty people died in the Jinja referral hospital in 2021 due to power cuts.[21] In the same year, it was reported that the Gulu regional referral hospital run short of oxygen due to power outages

[18] United Nations Development Programme: SDG 7 on Clean Energy. Can be accessed at https://www.undp.org/content/undp/en/home/sustainable-development-goals/goal-7-affordable-and-clean-energy.html.

[19] United Nations Development Programme: SDG 7 on Clean Energy. Can be accessed at https://www.undp.org/content/undp/en/home/sustainable-development-goals/goal-7-affordable-and-clean-energy.html.

[20] For a detailed discussion see, Nalule, V.R., *Energy Poverty and Access Challenges in Sub-Saharan Africa: The Role of Regionalism* (Springer, 2018).

[21] Monitor News, https://edition.cnn.com/2023/07/31/energy/sunak-north-sea-oil-gas-licenses/index.html. Last accessed on 1 August 2023.

experienced within the city.[22] Besides death in hospitals, indoor air pollution has also been reported to cause several deaths. For instance, in the Southern African Development Community (SADC) region, it has been reported that more than 153,000 people die each year from household pollution resulting from indoor burning of solid fuels such as traditional biomass for cooking and heating.[23] The link between energy access and the other UN SDGs has been elaborated in various literature.[24]

Taking cognisance of the above, therefore, it is clear that energy transition is influenced by various factors including geography; social and economic situation; political climate; availability of energy resources; the country's energy strategy. Recognizing the differences in societies, literature has flourished discussing terms such as energy justice, climate justice, environmental and the just transition.[25] Climate justice takes into account the need to share the benefits and burdens of climate change from a human rights perspective; energy justice refers to the application of human rights across the energy lifecycle[26]: and environmental justice aims to treat all citizens equally and to involve them in the development, implementation and enforcement of environmental laws, regulations and policies.[27]

Although the energy transition presents various opportunities including tackling climate change, job creation through investments in renewable energy and technological transfer: if not well managed, the

[22] The Independent, https://www.independent.co.ug/gulu-hospital-struggles-to-treat-patients-in-icu-over-power-outage/. Last accessed on 1 August 2023.

[23] Nalule, V.R., 'Regionalism in Addressing Energy Access Challenges' (2019) *Energy Poverty and Access Challenges in Sub-Saharan Africa: The Role of Regionalism*, 41–89.

[24] Nalule, V.R., 'How to Respond to Energy Transitions in Africa: Introducing the Energy Progression Dialogue' (2021) *Energy Transitions and the Future of the African Energy Sector: Law, Policy and Governance*, 3–5.

[25] Heffron, R.J. and McCauley, D., 'What Is 'Just Transition'?' (2018) 88 *Geoforum*, 74–77.

[26] Heffron, R.J., 'Applying Energy Justice into the Energy Transition' (2022) 156 *Renewable and Sustainable Energy Reviews*, 111936; and Heffron, R.J. and McCauley, D., 'The Concept of Energy Justice Across the Disciplines' (2017) 105 *Energy Policy*, 658–667.

[27] Heffron, R.J. and McCauley, D., 'What Is 'Just Transition'?' (2018) 88 *Geoforum*, 74–77.

energy transition could also escalate energy access and poverty challenges in the different countries across the globe.[28]

1.3 The Role of Extractives in the Energy Transition

The extractive industries includes oil, gas, coal and mineral extraction. Whereas fossil fuels are still playing a significant role in ensuring energy security in different countries, critical minerals on the other hand are crucial for the energy transition. Also included in the extractive industries are all the activities where citizens, corporations, governments, and financial institutions support the extraction of the resources.

As earlier stated, the extractive industries, especially the burning of fossil fuels are responsible for 75% of the global greenhouse gases, and nearly 90% of all carbon dioxide emissions.[29] And yet, it is not yet clear how much fossil fuels are used in the extraction of the critical minerals that are essential for the energy transition. Additionally, in recent years, it is evident that some countries are still dependent on fossil fuel revenue. For instance, it is reported that Saudi Arabia received as much as $326 billion in oil revenues during 2022; and the value of oil exports accounted for more than 70% of all Saudi exports in the same year.[30] In Norway, the estimated tax revenue from the oil and gas industry rose by 200% in 2022 to a record 884 billion Norwegian crowns ($89.3 billion).[31] In Trinidad, it is reported that the share of profit the country earned from production sharing contracts increased by 254% from $2.7 billion in 2021 to

[28] Nalule, V.R., 'How to Respond to Energy Transitions in Africa: Introducing the Energy Progression Dialogue' (2021) *Energy Transitions and the Future of the African Energy Sector: Law, Policy and Governance*, 3–35.

[29] United Nations: Climate Action, https://www.un.org/en/climatechange/science/causes-effects-climate-change#:~:text=Fossil%20fuels%20%E2%80%93%20coal%2C%20oil%20and,of%20all%20carbon%20dioxide%20emissions. Last accessed on 1 June 2023.

[30] Middle East Monitor, https://www.middleeastmonitor.com/20230222-saudi-oil-revenue-reach-326bn-highest-in-10-years/. Last accessed on 7 July 2023.

[31] Reuters, https://www.reuters.com/business/energy/norways-oil-gas-tax-revenue-soars-record-89-bln-2023-01-26/. Last accessed on 5 July 2023.

$9.6 billion in 2022: and that since 2018, T&T has earned $11.4 billion dollars in energy revenue from 2018 to the 3rd quarter of 2022.[32]

The above examples are evidence of the role of fossil fuels in revenue generation for different countries across the globe. Additionally, the geopolitics in Europe (Russia–Ukraine war), coupled with ineffective energy policies,[33] partly contributed to the global energy crisis. The finite nature of the extractive industry however, implies that countries must employ robust measures to protect the environment by, for example, ensuring mining closures and decommissioning at the end of the project life cycle.[34] The entire process of the extractives industry has an impact on the social, political, and economic sphere of the country.[35] In essence, the extractives industry comprises two main subsectors: petroleum and solid minerals. The processes in these sectors—for instance, oil and gas exploration, solid minerals mining, dredging, and quarrying—are associated with environmental concerns that directly affect the local communities and nearby landowners. Nevertheless, these activities are also responsible for the economic empowerment of various countries including the USA, UK, Norway, Saudi Arabia, Botswana to mention but a few.

1.4 The Scope of This Book

The purpose of this book therefore is to analyse how we can renegotiate extractive industry contracts in light of the ongoing energy transition. Law and the fiscal regime underpinning the extractive industry in a country are essential in determining the country's net-zero transition efforts. The fiscal regime basically refers to the set of instruments, laws,

[32] Caribbean Community, https://today.caricom.org/2022/11/14/trinidad-and-tobago-earns-11-8-billion-from-energy-revenues/#:~:text=The%20share%20of%20profit%20the,the%203rd%20quarter%20of%202022. Last accessed on 8 August 2023.

[33] Sokolowski, M.M. and Heffron, R.J., 'Defining and Conceptualising Energy Policy Failure: The When, Where, Why, and How' (2022) 161 *Energy Policy*, 112745; and Dr. Victoria R. Nalule, 'Ineffective Energy Policies', https://youtu.be/3k5E09ZkaGk. Last accessed on 10 October 2022.

[34] Heffron, R.J., 'The Role of Justice in Developing Critical Minerals' (2020) 7(3) *The Extractives Industry and Society*, 855–863; and Heffron, R.J., 'Energy Law for Decommissioning in the Energy Sector in the 21st Century' (2018) 11(3) *Journal of World Energy Law & Business*, 189–195.

[35] Olawuyi, D.S., *Extractives Industry Law in Africa* (Cham: Springer International Publishing, 2018).

regulations, agreements or tools that stipulate how revenues from oil, gas and mining activities are to be shared between the State and the extractive companies (ECs).[36] It should be realised that law is core to the energy sector as it sets the 'rules of the game'.[37] In the context of the extractive sector this is even more of the case as law sets the fiscal regime that for companies is fundamental to their decision-making process of whether to invest or not in construction and eventual operation plans. This book is therefore divided into five chapters, this being the introduction. Chapter 2 analyses the transition risks in extractive contracts. Chapter 3 reviews country case studies, to ascertain whether energy transitions have impacted extractive contracts. The penultimate Chapter 4 discusses the negotiation tools and strategies to address transition risks in extractive contracts. Finally, Chapter 5 gives the concluding remarks and an outlook for the future.

[36] Olawuyi, D.S., *Extractives Industry Law in Africa* (Springer International Publishing, 2018 September 11).

[37] Heffron, R.J., 'Energy Law in Crisis: An Energy Justice Revolution Is Needed' (2022) 15(3) *Journal of World Energy Law & Business*, 167–172.

CHAPTER 2

Energy Transition Risks in Contracts for the Extractive Industries

Abstract Risks have commonly been assessed and managed through the law. But with the climate change and energy access challenges, the view now is there is a new type of risk, and these can be referred to as 'justice' risks. These have been created by all the various factors affecting society today and have now transcended directly into the energy sector whereby they can be classed as key energy transition risks. In the past there has been a broad definition of risk in energy referred to as 'commercial risk'. This broad and clear definition is one that states commercial risk covers all risk except political risk, with political risk commonly understood as expropriation, adverse government action (including change in law or tax regime), and political or civil disturbance. This chapter therefore analyses the various energy transition risks, and spotlights how these could be mitigated, taking into cognizance the energy justice and just transition principles.

Keywords Energy transition risks · Climate change · Just transition · Energy justice · Extractives · Net zero

V. R. Nalule et al., *Renegotiating Contracts for the Energy Transition in the Extractives Industry*, Just Transitions,
https://doi.org/10.1007/978-3-031-46258-0_2

2.1 Risk in the Energy Sector

Conditions in society have been changing for multiple reasons, but the increase in data, the increased availability of technology, the financial crisis of 2007–2009, the COVID-19 pandemic, and now the 2020 financial crisis, and the recent Russia invasion of Ukraine have created what can be referred to as a '*perfect storm of energy justice*' whereby the opportunity for justice to permeate the energy sector has arisen; as Plato stated, '*Accidents and calamities … are the universal legislators of the world.*'

Risks have commonly been assessed and managed through the law. As stated above, the view now is there is a new type of risk, and these can be referred to as 'justice' risks. These have been created by all the various factors affecting society today and have now transcended directly into the energy sector whereby they can be classed as key energy transition risks. In the past there has been a broad definition of risk in energy referred to as 'commercial risk'. This broad and clear definition is one that states commercial risk covers all risk except political risk, with political risk commonly understood as expropriation, adverse government action (including change in law or tax regime), and political or civil disturbance.[1] The Russia invasion of Ukraine is a recent example of imposing significant political risk on businesses. A survey of companies with substantial international operations found that nearly 75% of them experienced a political risk loss in 2022. This represents a significant increase compared to the 35% of companies that faced similar losses in 2020.[2]

At the root of any assessment of risk is money in terms of costs of projects and finance. In terms of finance, at some point many state that commercial risk concerns repayment of finance, but again a broader understanding can be that commercial risk questions the viability of a project or activity. The different transition (justice) risks occur generally across four stages of a project and its associated activities, from planning to development to operation to the decommissioning stage. However,

[1] OECD, 'Commercial Risks Over the Project Life Cycle' (2020). https://rmid-oecd.asean.org/project-risks-mitigation/project-risks/commercial-risks/commercial-risks-over-the-project-life-cycle, accessed 20 December 2020.

[2] Oxford Analytica, 'How Are Global Businesses Managing Today's Political Risks?' (2023) https://pages.oxan.com/rs/109-ILL-989/images/2023-political-risk-survey-report.pdf, accessed 4 August 2023.

from the past it is clear that the decommissioning phase has not always been considered.[3]

In the context of the energy sector and this chapter,[4] commercial risk refers to energy projects in whichever stage they are at. It is proposed here that a definition of commercial risk has been lacking and that this is why there is a need for a concept of transition (justice) risks to be incorporated; this will ensure, for example, that the previously ignored issue of decommissioning is accounted for. However, more importantly, justice risks offer a more comprehensive approach to managing risk across a project's lifetime. When there is a stronger emphasis on justice, it leads to a notable decrease in commercial risk, compared to the previous approach that mainly focused on commercial risk during planning and construction phases.[5]

2.2 The Rise of Transition Risks in the Energy Sector

Irrespective of COVID-19 and the Russia's war of aggression against Ukraine 2020 financial crisis, the energy transition has been underway,[6] and that is clear both from energy research and practitioner literature. Even the latter event has prompted some initiatives, like the EU plan,

[3] Heffron, R.J., 'Energy Law for Decommissioning in the Energy Sector in the 21st Century' (2018) 11(3) *Journal of World Energy Law & Business*, 189.

[4] Overall, this chapter says thanks to the Journal of Energy and Natural Resources Law for reproducing parts of the text in an open-access journal and from the author Raphael Heffron and it has been updated and modified: Heffron, R., Connor, R., Crossley, P., Mayor, V.L.-I., Talus, K., and Tomain, J. 2021. 'The Identification and Impact of Justice Risks to Commercial Risks in the Energy Sector: Post COVID-19 and for the Energy Transition' (2021) 39(4) *Journal of Energy & Natural Resources Law*, 439–468.

[5] Heffron, Raphael J., and De Fontenelle, Louis, 'Implementing Energy Justice Through a New Social Contract' (2023) 41(2) *Journal of Energy & Natural Resources Law*, 141–155.

[6] Directorate-General for Communication (European Commission), 'The EU in 2022: General Report on the Activities of the European Union' (2023), https://op.europa.eu/en/publication-detail/-/publication/d73b364e-c180-11ed-8912-01aa75ed71a1/language-en, accessed 5 August 2023.

REPowerEU, to accelerate energy transition more seriously.[7] However, what has been evolving is the role for justice in that transition and how it will be achieved.[8] With greater justice, there will be a reduction in commercial risk.[9] Generally, the search for justice is driven by a need to rebalance a relationship that has become unbalanced.[10] That is why governments, companies, and individuals enter into contracts. It is also why one goes to court, to ensure compensation or behavioural change as a result of an imbalanced relationship. In this context, what is in essence at stake is that an individual's or group's rights are being infringed. To avoid going to court, the parties will enter into a contract.

In this case, they will enter into the contract to avoid these energy transition risks in the extractives industry; it should be noted however that these risks will apply across the energy sector too, and later chapters will cover in more detail some of the energy transition risks more specific and important to the extractives industry.

Legal theory today highlights the different drivers of energy law (or evolution of energy law) and how we are in a phase where infrastructure and justice are the key drivers of the formulation of energy law, as opposed to issues such as economics, security and safety.[11] This demand for infrastructure and justice are in essence encapsulated in the energy transition which is transforming society. It has also increased demand for new projects, specifically on critical minerals in the extractives industry.

Indeed, leading interdisciplinary energy and energy law journals which have had special issues on 'justice', such as *Nature Energy* (2016), *Energy Policy* (2017), *Applied Energy* (2018), *Journal of Human Development*

[7] EU Commission, 'REPowerEU Affordable, Secure and Sustainable Energy for Europe' (2022), https://commission.europa.eu/strategy-and-policy/priorities-2019-2024/european-green-deal/repowereu-affordable-secure-and-sustainable-energy-europe_en, accessed 6 August 2023.

[8] Heffron, R.J., and McCauley, D., 'What Is the "Just Transition"?' (2018) 88 *Geoforum*, 74–77; McCauley, D., and Heffron, R.J., 'Just Transition: Integrating Climate, Energy and Environmental Justice' (2018) 119 *Energy Policy*, 1.

[9] De Goër de Herve, Mathilde, Schinko, Thomas, and Handmer, John, 'Risk Justice: Boosting the Contribution of Risk Management to Sustainable Development' (2023) *Risk Analysis*, https://doi.org/10.1111/risa.14157.

[10] This premise is from Heffron OIES—Heffron, R.J., 'Justice in the Energy Transition. Special Issue: 'Decarbonisation Pathways for Oil and Gas' (2020) March (121) The Oxford Institute for Energy Studies.

[11] Heffron and Talus (n. 1).

and Capabilities (2021), and *Journal of World Energy Law and Business* (2023). In addition, there has been a notable and significant rise in the influential economics literature in terms of justice issues. Economics since the 2007–2009 financial crisis has started to engage with this issue in a significant way (one can follow the work of leading economists such as Joseph Stiglitz [2012], Thomas Piketty [2015], Walter Scheidel [2017] and Anthony Atkinson [2015]).[12] Indeed, Thomas Piketty, in his recent book *Capital and Ideology* (2020, 670), decries the issue and states that despite living in a world of big data, public data on inequality is inadequate. Piketty (2020) notes the key issue of inequality and climate change emissions, and from this perspective he highlights how this will cost economies (and more likely developing ones) 5–20% of global gross domestic product (GDP); and further he cites the Stern Review (2007) and the Intergovernmental Panel on Climate Change (IPCC 2018) report, demonstrating that these effects may be accelerated as a result of pollution and environmental damage since 2007.[13]

The core justice principles are well-documented in the literature and these can be summarized in brief as below:

- *Distributive justice* focuses on burdens, risks, costs and benefits;
- *Procedural justice* assesses government and public decision-making and processes;
- *Restorative justice* aims to rectify or ameliorate existing harms or injustices;
- *Recognition justice* aims to ensure that all social groups participate in decision-making; and
- *Cosmopolitan justice* focuses on the impact of actions taken in one country on people in other countries.

[12] Piketty, T., Capital in the Twenty-First Century (Goldhammer, A., Belknap Press of Harvard University Press, 2014); Tirole, J., *Economics for the Common Good* (Princeton University Press, 2017); Scheidel, W., *The Great Leveler* (Princeton University Press, 2017); Stiglitz, J.E., *The Price of Inequality* (Penguin Books, 2012); Atkinson, A.B., *Inequality: What Can Be Done?* (Harvard University Press, 2015).

[13] Piketty, T., Capital and Ideology (A Goldhammer tr, Belknap Press of Harvard University Press, 2020); IPCC, Summary for Policymakers (2018). In: Global warming of 1.5 °C.; Stern, N.H., & Great Britain. *The Economics of Climate Change: The Stern Review* (Cambridge, UK: Cambridge University Press, 2007).

Justice risks are the risks that result from society seeking more fairness, inclusive-ness and equitable solutions, and resolving inequality in a variety of ways. In essence, they aim to address a normative situation—*the way society wants the world to be*—to provide a future pathway for societal development. With the energy transition focusing on a just transition, these can be referred to as energy transition risks which we advance here as the key fundamental transition risks for the extractives industry. These transition risks can be legislated for or contracted for and just outcomes can be improved in society. At the core improving the contract should be the elements of justice above and by so doing, the energy transition risk will be improved. We identify 12 transition risks, and these are discussed in turn in the section.

2.3 Energy Transition Risks for the Extractive Industries

In this section, each risk is identified and discussed in turn. This list is not exhaustive however, we advance that the majority of risks will fall in under these 12 categories. Further, these risks are focused on projects as they are planned, constructed, operated and decommissioned, in essence as they go through the project life-cycle. As stated earlier, to improve the management of these risks must be based on 'justice' so that just outcomes are improved for the energy sector and more broadly society. The five justice principles provide a basis for improving the risk management process and these justice principles will result in the risk been managed for the medium to long-term (rather than a short term profit making focus).

2.3.1 The Economic Risk

Inequality is widening, posing major moral, social, and political challenges to which policymakers must react. The World Inequality Report 2022 reveals that the bottom 50% of the global population possesses 2% of the total global wealth, while the top 10% holds 76%. Over the period from 1995 to 2021, the top 1% garnered 38% of the incremental global wealth, and the global top 0.1% experienced a rise from 7 to 11%. Since 1995, billionaires' share of global wealth has grown from 1% to over

3%, with the COVID pandemic causing the sharpest increase in 2020.[14] Abhijit Banerjee and Esther Duflo (2019 Nobel Prize winners) highlight how inequality reduced globally from 1950 to 1980, even as Western nations experienced rapid growth. This counters the idea that fast growth requires inequality. High taxes and shared inequality control beliefs played roles. However, a shift in the US and UK towards valuing private wealth accumulation increased inequality, affecting nations like India and China. Policy changes further elevated inequality.[15]

There is an increasing consensus among economists more than ever that inequality is restraining economic growth by reducing economic opportunities for the lower and middle classes and fostering (or reflecting) monopolistic rents for the very wealthy and that inequality is a first-order problem requiring significant policy attention.[16] There has been an increased focus on inequality, for example in Thomas Piketty's Capital in the Twenty-First Century,[17] and Jean Tirole, a Nobel Prize-winning economist, stated in essence, in his book in Economics for the Common Good,[18] that justice (via law) has a key role to play in ensuring that society can address the issues of the energy and climate crisis.

Changes to laws and government policy have increasingly begun to address issues of inequality across all parts of our societies, including the energy sector. A government can enhance the economic standing of a particular beneficiary or group of beneficiaries to achieve a particular purpose—for example, a policy of granting subsidies to owners of renewable energy assets in order to incentivise investment in such assets, thereby accelerating the growth of such low-carbon power generation and reducing carbon emissions. It is a form of procedural justice. The latest IPCC report, the Sixth Assessment Report, confidently states that various ways to reduce emissions are getting cheaper due to a combination of government policies. These policies involve investing in research

[14] World Inequality Lab, 'World Inequality Report 2022' (2023), https://wir2022.wid.world/, accessed 7 August 2023.

[15] Ibid.: World Inequality Lab, 'World Inequality Report 2022' (2023), https://wir2022.wid.world/, accessed 7 August 2023.

[16] Blanchard, Olivier, and Rodrik, Dani, *Combating Inequality: Rethinking Government's Role* (MIT Press, 2021), xi– xiii.

[17] See eg Piketty (n. 15).

[18] Tirole (n. 15).

and development (R&D), funding tests and pilot projects, and giving incentives like subsidies to promote wider use of cleaner technology.[19]

It has been argued that the role of government in transitioning to a sustainable economy includes: (1) funding for science-based research; (2) using fiscal policy to mobilise private capital into low-carbon investments; (3) public investment in sustainable infrastructure; (4) regulating behaviours to limit damage to and destruction of ecosystems; (5) partnering with the private sector; (6) measuring and monitoring progress towards sustainability targets; and (7) transferring sustainable technologies to developing countries.[20]

Fundamentally, however, the energy transition is a matter of energy policy. Broadbased policy support is the premise of all other forms of government support. And with 197 countries having signed the Paris Agreement therefore broad political support appears to exist in abundance. Nevertheless, grand and ambitious declarations remain mere expressions of intent unless underpinned by detailed and comprehensive policy package and measures aimed at realizing these commitments. Having comprehensive and detailed policies becomes even more evident when reminded that the transition must be just, fair, inclusive, and adaptable to events that could impede its progress. For instance, the ongoing energy crisis triggered by Russia's invasion of Ukraine has challenged many national transition policies. Governments, in order to shield consumers, often resorted to the simplest approach of introducing new fossil fuel subsidies to counter energy price increases.[21] However, these actions frequently did not target assistance to those in need or receive support from additional measures facilitating their participation in the shift to clean energy. This is the reason why many international organizations such as IEA, World Economic Forum, IRENA, and others that

[19] IPCC, 'Climate Change 2023: Synthesis Report', https://www.ipcc.ch/assessment-report/ar6/, accessed 7 August 2023.

[20] Cohen, Steven, *The Role of Government in the Transition to a Sustainable Economy*. Huffpost, 12 April 2014.

[21] IEA, 'Fossil Fuel Consumption Subsidies 2022' (2023), https://www.iea.org/reports/fossil-fuels-consumption-subsidies-2022, https://www.iea.org/reports/fossil-fuels-consumption-subsidies-2022, accessed 8 August 2023.

monitor and promote the transition have updated their policy packages after the recent energy crisis triggered by Russia's invasion of Ukraine.[22]

The Paris Agreement reflects a significant display of multilateral cooperation, yet its success relies on individual nations pursuing their own carbon reduction strategies. Evaluating progress and pending tasks is contingent on a country-specific basis. For example, the UK Government has multiple policies focused on curbing greenhouse gas emissions, responsible for climate change. The central document outlining its climate change strategy is the Net Zero Strategy (Build Back Greener), released on October 19, 2021, and subsequently updated in April 2022. It outlines strategies and suggestions for decarbonizing all sectors of the UK economy to achieve the government's net zero goal by 2050. This strategy builds upon the Ten-point plan for a green industrial revolution, introduced on November 18, 2020. On July 18, 2022, the English High Court ruled that the UK's Net Zero Strategy, challenged by Friends of the Earth and others, was insufficient to achieve the country's 2050 net zero goals. The court ordered the government to publish more detailed policies that show how the UK's carbon budgets would be met by March 2023.[23] Thus in March 2023, the government updated the policy with a series of publications grouped under the policy paper titled "Powering Up Britain".[24]

[22] IEA, 'World Energy Outlook 2022' (2022), https://www.iea.org/reports/world-energy-outlook-2022/energy-security-in-energy-transitions, accessed 8 August 2023; World Economic Forum, 'Securing the Energy Transition' (2023), https://www.weforum.org/whitepapers/securing-the-energy-transition/, accessed 8 August 2023, & IRENA, 'World Energy Transitions Outlook 2022: 1.5 °C Pathway' (2022), https://www.irena.org/publications/2022/mar/world-energy-transitions-outlook-2022, accessed 8 August 2023.

[23] R (Friends of the Earth Ltd and ors) v Secretary of State for Business, Energy and Industrial Strategy [2022] EWHC 1841 (Admin), available at https://www.judiciary.uk/wp-content/uploads/2022/07/FoE-v-BEIS-judgment-180722.pdf, accessed 8 August 2023.

[24] Carver, Dominic, and Walker, Alan, 'Research Briefing: Government Policy on Reaching Net Zero by 2050' (2023), https://commonslibrary.parliament.uk/research-briefings/cdp-2023-0124/, accessed 8 August 2023.

The Powering Up Britain bundle consists of the Energy Security Plan,[25] Net Zero Growth Plan,[26] and Carbon Budget Delivery Plan.[27] Additionally, the government introduced the 2023 Green Finance Strategy, aimed at facilitating the required financial support for the UK's net zero, energy security, and nature-driven economies.[28] The Nature Markets Framework was also unveiled to encourage private sector involvement in channeling green finance towards nature-related initiatives.[29] This collection of detailed policies has established a relatively comprehensive framework for the UK's energy transition, with the nature of support differing for each initiative.

The governments of some other countries have gone even further to support the energy transition. However, not all countries have gone as far. A few countries like Iran have not yet ratified the Paris Agreement[30] and the commitments of other major emitters including China, Russia and Saudi Arabia have been criticised as insufficient to achieve the objectives of the Paris Agreement.[31] The latest IPCC report clearly and confidently stated that any further delay in concerted global climate action will miss a brief and rapidly closing window of opportunity to secure a liveable and

[25] HM Government, 'Powering Up Britain: Energy Security Plan' (March 2023), https://assets.publishing.service.gov.uk/government/uploads/system/uploads/attachment_data/file/1148252/powering-up-britain-energy-security-plan.pdf, accessed 8 August 2023.

[26] HM Government, 'Powering Up Britain: Net Zero Growth Plan' (March 2023), https://assets.publishing.service.gov.uk/government/uploads/system/uploads/attachment_data/file/1147457/powering-up-britain-net-zero-growth-plan.pdf, accessed 8 July 2023.

[27] HM Government, 'Carbon Budget Delivery Plan' (March 2023), https://www.gov.uk/government/publications/carbon-budget-delivery-plan, accessed 8 August 2023.

[28] HM Government, 'Mobilising Green Investment: 2023 Green Finance Strategy' (March 2023), https://www.gov.uk/government/publications/green-finance-strategy, accessed 8 August 2023.

[29] HM Government, 'Nature Markets: A Framework for Scaling Up Private Investment in Nature Recovery and Sustainable Farming' (March 2023), https://www.gov.uk/government/publications/nature-markets, accessed 8 August 2023.

[30] UNDP, 'Global Climate Promise: Iran' (2022), https://climatepromise.undp.org/what-we-do/where-we-work/iran, accessed 8 August 2023.

[31] See profiles and analysis of countries' commitments at https://climateactiontracker.org/, accessed 8 August 2023.

sustainable future for all.[32] The world had not yet recovered from the shock of the global COVID-19 pandemic when Russia's War on Ukraine began, causing many countries to face an energy crisis. Some fear that the political momentum behind the energy transition will be lost when facing these global challenges, and that carbon reduction measures will be deemed unnecessary expenses as recessions bite and energy crises unfold.

2.3.2 *Taxation Risk*

Tackling 21st-century challenges requires addressing income and wealth inequalities through significant redistribution. The emergence of contemporary welfare states during the twentieth century, marked by significant advancements in healthcare, education, and equal opportunities, was connected to the increase in highly progressive tax rates.[33] The government's ability to track how people and corporations earn and spend money has enabled the gradual rise in taxes, including those related to earnings, profits, wages, and the value of goods, all connected to corresponding patterns of income and spending. Before the twentieth century, the government could only tax property and a few specific goods.[34] Today, even though advanced technology enables governments to monitor individuals' and businesses' financial activities more effectively, multinational corporations can still avoid paying corporate taxes by moving their profits to low-tax countries. Taxation in the extractives industry is vitally important and also a key risk in the energy transition as revenues from fossil fuels may decrease and critical minerals may rise.

The use of tax havens is now well documented, and there have been major leaks that have promoted change (the Panama Papers, the

[32] IPCC, 'Climate Change 2023: Synthesis Report', https://www.ipcc.ch/assessment-report/ar6/, accessed 7 August 2023.

[33] (n. 18) World Inequality Lab.

[34] Piketty, Thomas, and Saez, Emmanuel, 'Optimal Labor Income Taxation' in Auerbach, Alan J., and others (eds) *Handbook of Public Economics Volume 5* (OUP, 2013), 394.

Pandora Papers, and the Paradise Papers).[35] Consequently, greater attention is currently focused on international transactions, particularly because energy companies were exposed as heavy users of tax havens. The Organisation for Economic Co-operation and Development (OECD) is aiming, through several initiatives, to examine the issues (particularly inequality) whereby the unfair world of international taxation[36] is causing injustice in the energy sector (and especially in the mining sector).[37]

New advancements in global taxation demonstrate that achieving more equitable economic policies is feasible both on a worldwide scale and within individual nations. Although the fundamental role of tax policy is to collect money to pay for government spending, much discussion nowadays is framed around an alternative, corrective role for taxation.[38] The concept of using taxation to correct negative externalities such as pollution is generally credited to Pigou (1920), and such corrective taxes are sometimes called Pigouvian Taxation.[39] The core concept is straightforward: negative externalities occur when the production or consumption of a certain commodity causes harm to individuals beyond the immediate buyer or seller involved. Such instances represent a market failure, as the decisions made by these buyers and sellers don't account for the additional costs imposed on others.

[35] See all three of the following: Obermayer, B., and Obermaier, F., *The Panama Papers*. OneWorld Publications, 2016; Shaxson, N., *Treasure Island*. Penguin, Random House 2016—Original edition 2011; and EU Parliament, 'The Pandora Papers' (2022), https://www.europarl.europa.eu/committees/en/the-pandora-papers/product-details/20220830CDT10062#20220830CDT10062-section-0.

[36] Heffron, R.J., and Sheehan, J., 'Rethinking International Taxation and Energy Policy Post COVID-19 and the Financial Crisis for Developing Countries' (2020) 38(4) *Journal of Energy & Natural Resources Law*, 465.

[37] Heffron, R.J., 'The Application of Distributive Justice to Energy Taxation Utilising Sovereign Wealth Funds' (2018) 122 *Energy Policy*, 649; Heffron, R.J., 'The Role of Justice in Developing Critical Minerals' (2020) 7(3) *The Extractives Industry and Society*, 855–863; and Qurbani, I.D., Heffron, R.J., and Rifano, A.T.S., 'Justice and Critical Mineral Development in Indonesia and Across ASEAN' (2021). *The Extractives Industry and Society, Advance Access*, https://doi.org/10.1016/j.exis.2020.11.017.

[38] Kopczuk, Wojciech, 'Reflections on Taxation in Support of Redistributive Policies' in Blanchard, Olivier, and Rodrik, Dani, *Combating Inequality: Rethinking Government's Role* (MIT Press, 2021), 255.

[39] Williams, Roberton C., 'Environmental Taxation' in Auerbach, Alan J., and Smetters Kent (eds), The Economics of Tax Policy (OUP, 2017), 50.

If the latter tax is based on the harm caused by a product to others, it makes sure the buyer pays for that harm. This encourages the market to make the right amount of the product, considering its impact on society. One of the most significant instances of this type of taxation is Carbon Pricing, which is considered an essential component of an efficient emissions reduction strategy.[40] This carbon pricing is also a matter of fairness, as it becomes evident that the lowest 50% of the global population emit an average of 1.6 tonnes per year, contributing to 12% of the total emissions, while the top 10% emit 31 tonnes, accounting for around 47.6% of the total emissions.[41]

Although the design of carbon pricing schemes may differ based on specific policy goals and contexts, effective schemes share common traits. The FASTER Principles for Successful Carbon Pricing, a guide collaboratively developed by the World Bank and the Organisation for Economic Co-operation and Development (OECD), distills six crucial attributes for successful carbon pricing including fairness, transparency, alignment of policies and objectives, stability and predictability, efficiency and cost-effectiveness, reliability and environmental integrity.[42]

Furthermore, the reporting of taxation, the amount paid, its sources, and the handling of potential tax revenue will be crucial matters to consider. Distributive justice will gain greater significance in the future as society strives to restore fairness in both national and global tax systems and address human rights violations arising from inequitable international tax agreements.[43] Taxation will be a vital transition risk to be managed in the energy transition and the focus should clearly be on having the principle of distributive justice at its core of any contract re-negotiation.

[40] Stiglitz, Joseph and others, *Report of the High-Level Commission on Carbon Prices* (World Bank, 2017), https://doi.org/10.7916/d8-w2nc-4103, accessed 9 August 2023.

[41] (n. 18) World Inequality Lab, 'World Inequality Report 2022' (2023), https://wir2022.wid.world/, accessed 7 August 2023.

[42] Carbon Pricing Leadership Coalition, 'What Is Carbon Pricing', https://www.carbonpricingleadership.org/what, accessed 9 August 2023.

[43] Heffron, R.J., and Sheehan, J., 'Rethinking International Taxation and Energy Policy Post COVID-19 and the Financial Crisis for Developing Countries' (2020) 38(4) *Journal of Energy & Natural Resources Law*, 465.

2.3.3 Project Finance Risk in the Energy Transition

Project finance has been described as 'the most widespread financial technique that financial markets have developed for the participation of private capital in unlisted infrastructure …'.[44] In and of itself, however, project finance has been in the past climate agnostic—it is best suited simply to whichever projects ensure and secure stable revenues over the long term. However, in light of the established and definite scientific understanding regarding the role of burning fossil fuels in climate change, providing financial backing for any kind of fossil fuel projects, including project finance, seems to raise questions of distributive justice.

During COP 26, 34 countries and five public finance institutions pledged to cease international public finance (IPF) for fossil fuels and instead prioritize public finance for clean energy by the end of 2022, signing the Statement on International Public Support for the Clean Energy Transition (the "Glasgow Statement").[45] Although the Glasgow Statement is not explicitly about project financing, its successful implementation could directly shift USD 28 billion in international public finance for fossil fuels toward a clean and just energy transition each year.[46] However, a recent study from IISD reveals that many of the countries that agreed to the Glasgow Statement haven't yet put in place strong plans and rules to stop funding fossil fuels and promote clean energy in a way that aligns with the goals of the statement.[47]

The World Bank issued the first labelled green bond in 2008, and today, in addition to its green bond program, issues USD 40–50 billion in Sustainable Development Bonds annually to support the financing of a combination of green and social, i.e., "sustainable development" projects,

[44] Della Croce, Raffaele and Gatti, Stefano, 'Financing Infrastructure—International Trends' 2014 (1).

OECD Journal: Financial Market Trends.

[45] COP 26 (2021) Statement on International Public Support for the Clean Energy Transition, https://webarchive.nationalarchives.gov.uk/ukgwa/20230313124743/https://ukcop26.org/statement-on-international-public-support-for-the-clean-energy-transition/, accessed 10 August 2023.

[46] IISD, 'Countries Could Shift Almost USD 28 Billion/Year from Fossil Fuels to Jump-Start the Energy Transition—If They Follow Through on Their Pledges' (2022) https://www.iisd.org/articles/press-release/glasgow-statement-could-shift-annual-28-billion-to-clean, accessed 10 August 2023.

[47] IISD, 'Turning Pledges in to Action' (2022), https://www.iisd.org/publications/report/turning-glasgow-statement-into-action, accessed 10 August 2023.

programs, and activities in middle-income countries.[48] Globally, issuers sold $487.1 billion worth of green bonds in 2022, which shows an increase of 67% since 2020.[49] In the absence of regulation, the market responded with the emergence of voluntary standards, such as the Green Bond Principles and the Climate Bond Standards, against which issuers can have their issuances accredited by independent environmental rating agencies.

Policymakers are now catching up; in 2020 the EU has passed a regulation on the establishment of a framework to facilitate sustainable investment known as the Taxonomy Regulation. The EU Taxonomy Regulation (2020/852/EU) creates an EU-wide classification system for environmentally sustainable economic activities. The regulation contains some objectives, designed to support the EU's Green New Deal and 2030 climate and energy targets.[50] In June 3, 2023 the European Commission has put forward a new sustainable finance package which encompasses several documents: a new legislative proposal on Environmental, Social and Governance (ESG) rating agencies, a recommendation on transition finance, and a staff working document on the Taxonomy usability. Furthermore, it includes the final Delegated Act on Taxonomy criteria, known as the Environmental Taxonomy, which plays a crucial role in classifying activities as sustainable based on their impacts on climate, biodiversity, marine and freshwater ecosystems, pollution, and the circular economy.[51]

Green bonds are undoubtedly providing a major source of funding for a transition to a low-carbon economy, however, in most cases they are not a source of project finance in the true sense. Most green bonds are treasury bonds issued against the balance sheet of large financial institutions, governments and corporations. For the development of individual energy

[48] World Bank, 'Sovereign Green, Social, and Sustainability Bonds Set to Grow as Emerging Markets Focus on Sustainability' (2022), https://www.worldbank.org/en/news/press-release/2022/11/07/sovereign-green-social-and-sustainability-bonds-set-to-grow-as-emerging-markets-focus-on-sustainability, accessed 10 August 2023.

[49] See, for example www.climatebonds.net, accessed 20 December 2020.

[50] European Commission, 'EU Taxonomy for Sustainable Activities', https://finance.ec.europa.eu/sustainable-finance/tools-and-standards/eu-taxonomy-sustainable-activities_en, accessed 10 August 2023.

[51] European Commission, 'Sustainable Finance Package', https://finance.ec.europa.eu/publications/sustainable-finance-package-2023_en, accessed 10 August 2023.

projects, loans—from both commercial lenders and development finance institutions—remain the dominant source of debt finance.[52] Similar to the Green Bond Principles, the Green Loan Principles are also optional. However, the growth of regulations, policies, and market norms related to green bonds indicates a growing requirement for banks and financial institutions to reveal more about environmental sustainability and climate risk. This could encourage financial institutions to possess loans that are certified as 'green' by independent bodies. Considering the trend in the green bond market, we can anticipate a swift increase in green loan funding, which might have a crucial role in facilitating a fair transition to clean energy.

2.3.4 Bankruptcy Risks in the Energy Transition

Financial underperformance is on the rise in the energy sector with the ongoing energy transition.[53] Many would argue that it has been an issue in energy companies, which have tried to avoid environmental responsibilities.[54] Bankruptcy in the energy sector is on the rise. Only in the North America 20 oil and gas producers filed for bankruptcy in 2021.[55] In the EU, a potential, short-term threat to its supply security has been recognised as the bankruptcy of a major energy supplier in the EU. This could trigger a chain reaction of financial challenges in both the energy sector and the broader European economy. Bruegel's September 2022

[52] Climate Bond Initiative, 'Sustainable Debt Global State of the Market 2022', https://www.climatebonds.net/files/reports/cbi_sotm_2022_03e.pdf, accessed 10 August 2023.

[53] See the dramatic fall in General Electric, the US company charted in the following book: Gryta, T., and Mann, T., *Lights Out: Pride, Delusion and the Fall of General Electric* (Houghton Mifflin Harcourt, 2020).

[54] (n. 8). Heffron, R.J., 'Energy Law for Decommissioning in the Energy Sector in the 21st Century' (2018) 11(3) *Journal of World Energy Law & Business*, 189.

[55] Boone, Haynes, 'Oil Patch Bankruptcy Monitor' (2022), https://www.haynesboone.com/-/media/project/haynesboone/haynesboone/pdfs/energy_bankruptcy_reports/oil_patch_bankruptcy_monitor.pdf?rev=e57d3129b7504ea190df5d33dbacae44&hash=F461E4FE13446BE821B8AE9080C349E6, accessed 10 August 2023.

report cautions against this situation, highlighting that certain Member States have a single dominant player in their energy market.[56]

More importantly, there are ongoing climate risks for companies. In the past, corporations have addressed climate change through Corporate Social Responsibility (CSR) to uphold their reputation. Yet, the bankruptcy of Pacific Gas & Electric (PG&E), the largest electric company in California, in January 2019 underscored the serious financial threat that climate-related bankruptcy can poses to companies.[57] The wildfires leveled California towns, destroying 19,000 homes and causing over $30 billion in damage. PG&E settled for $13.5 million with wildfire victims[58] and faced 84 criminal charges of involuntary manslaughter with a $4 million fine.[59] While PG&E is investor-owned, climate costs burden state, local governments, ratepayers, and taxpayers, extending beyond private utilities. This disaster has been termed the first climate change bankruptcy in the world with the human loss incalculable.

Climate risks are split into two types: physical and transition risks. Physical risks come from the actual impacts of climate change, like extreme weather (acute) and long-term shifts (chronic) such as rising sea levels or sustained higher temperatures. These can lead to damage and disruptions in supply chains, affecting organizations financially. More specifically, the transition risks which are business risks that come with changes as society and the economy move to being more climate-friendly. Power utilities, as a major contributor to greenhouse gas (GHG) are early and logical targets for GHG reductions across society.[60] These risks include things like policy changes, new technologies, market shifts, reputation worries, and legal matters. They're all connected and are a big concern for investors

[56] EU Parliament, 'Four Challenges of the Energy Crisis for the EU's Strategic Autonomy' (2023), https://www.europarl.europa.eu/RegData/etudes/BRIE/2023/747099/EPRS_BRI(2023)747099_EN.pdf, accessed 10 August 2023.

[57] Wyman, Oliver, 'Climate Change: Managing a New Financial Risk' (2019), https://www.oliverwyman.com/content/dam/oliver-wyman/v2/publications/2019/feb/Oliver_Wyman_Climate_Change_Managing_A_New_Financial_Risk_paper.pdf, accessed 11 August 2023.

[58] Morris, J.D., Fire Victims Seek Assurances on PG&E's $13.5 Billion Bankruptcy Deal. *San Francisco Chronicle*, 6 April 2020.

[59] Avalos, George, PG&E Pleads Guilty to Criminal Charges in Fatal 2018 Camp Fire in Butte County. *The Mercury News*, 23 March 2020.

[60] TCFD, 'Climate Radar' (2018), https://www.tcfdhub.org/wp-content/uploads/2019/07/Climate-Change-and-Power-Utilites-Final.pdf, accessed 11 August 2023.

trying to manage their assets in a world focused on cutting carbon. For asset managers and investors, figuring out how much transition risk their portfolio has can be quite challenging.[61]

Utilities can adopt diverse investment strategies to mitigate risks and future liabilities. Internally, it's crucial to mandate environmental planning, risk assessment, and resilience planning. Furthermore, utilities must rethink their business models. The practice of constructing massive central power stations, especially those reliant on fossil fuels, needs revision. Indeed, ignoring climate change and not investing in resilience could lead to even more financial risks.

2.3.5 *Disclosure and Transparency Risks*

The significance of enhancing transparency within the extractive industries to better govern the sector, reduce corruption, illicit financial flows, and address the challenges of the "resource curse" has long been widely recognized.[62] While enhanced transparency regarding payments to foreign governments and similar details constitutes positive progress, it simultaneously introduces heightened risks for energy sector enterprises. For example, the international Extractive Industries Transparency Initiative (EITI) requires signatory states and investors to disclose the details of their taxation relationship, beneficial owners of companies and so on, with the EITI Secretariat monitoring the submissions. Indeed, a major focus of EITI in 2023 has been a renewed focus on transparency.

Numerous emerging legal tools are being adopted by countries to enhance disclosure and openness. However, many of these tools also introduce added risks for energy firms. The 'social licence to operate' (SLO—the relationship between energy corporations and the local community, which is becoming formalised through a contract) requires more transparency between an energy project developer and the local community, and some projects have been stopped when the terms of

[61] EPA, 'Climate Risks and Opportunities Defined' (2022), https://www.epa.gov/climateleadership/climate-risks-and-opportunities-defined, accessed 11 August 2023.

[62] OECD, 'Governing Through Transparency: Addressing Corruption, Accountability, and Illicit Financial Flows in Oil Trading' (2023), https://www.oecd.org/dac/corruption-accountability-illicit-financial-flows-oil-countries.pdf, accessed 12 August 2023.

the licence were not honoured, for example in high-profile cases in Colombia.[63]

The topic of voluntary nonfinancial Environmental, Social, and Governance (ESG) disclosure is experiencing rapid growth and rising significance. This subject has garnered considerable interest from both academic scholars and participants in capital markets over the past few years.[64] Although ESG factors are not a new concept, there is no single universal definition of ESG factors, nor is there a single definition of ESG risks or their types.[65] ESG can be defined as '*criteria [that] are a set of standards for a company's operations that socially conscious investors use to screen potential investments. Environmental criteria consider how a company performs as a steward of nature*'.[66] Unlike the traditional or normal corporate disclosures, ESG has its focus on non-financial disclosures.[67] According to the World Bank, Sovereign ESG Data Framework, ESG includes:

- E: the Environment pillar assesses a country's economic sustainability by considering its natural resources, management practices, climate resilience, and environmental impacts from economic activities, with a focus on internalizing externalities, sustainable energy access, and food security, all pivotal for enduring economic growth.
- S: the Social pillar evaluates a country's economic sustainability by assessing its effectiveness in fulfilling its population's basic needs, alleviating poverty, addressing social and equity concerns, and

[63] Heffron, R.J., and others, 'The Emergence of the "Social Licence to Operate" in the Extractive Industries?' (2018) *Resources Policy*, https://doi.org/10.1016/j.resourpol.2018.09.012.

[64] Tsang, Albert, Frost, Tracie, and Cao, Huijuan, 'Environmental, Social, and Governance (ESG) Disclosure: A Literature Review' (2023) 55(1) *The British Accounting Review*, https://doi.org/10.1016/j.bar.2022.101149.

[65] Ziolo, Magdalena, and Spoz, Anna, 'ESG Risk in Financial Decisions of Financial Markets and Companies' in Ziolo, Magdalena, Escrig-Olmedo, Elena, and Rodrigo, Lozano (eds), *Fostering Sustainable Business Models Through Financial Markets* (Springer, 2022), 92.

[66] Investopedia (2020) ESG, www.investopedia.com/terms/e/environmental-social-and-governance-esg-criteria.asp, accessed 20 December 2020.

[67] Brest, Paul, Gilson, Ronald J., and Wolfson, Mark A., 'Essay: How Investors Can (and Can't) Create Social Value' (2018) 44 *Journal of Corporation Law* 205, at 211.

investing in human capital and productivity, encompassing demographic factors essential for stable long-term economic growth.; and

- G: the Governance pillar describes the sustainability of a country's economic performance in the context of its institutional capacity to support long-term stability, growth and poverty reduction. This category also accounts for the strength of a country's political, financial and legal systems and capacity to address environmental and social risks.[68]

Various ESG disclosure obligations are rapidly becoming more prevalent in home states of major energy companies. The European Union, South Africa, Singapore, Hong Kong, and the United Kingdom, among others, have instituted specific sustainability reporting regulations.[69] The European Union has taken a leading role in ESG disclosure obligations, require large companies and listed companies to publish regular reports on the social and environmental risks they face, and on how their activities impact people and the environment.[70]

The European Union (EU) Directive on Non-Financial Reporting (2014/95/EU) requires certain large companies to provide a non-financial statement containing information to the extent necessary for an understanding of the undertaking's development, performance, position and impact of its activity, relating to, at minimum, environmental, social and employee matters, respect for human rights, anti-corruption and bribery matters.[71] The European Commission approved the Corporate Sustainability Reporting Directive on April 21, 2021. This directive significantly broadens the climate details that covered companies are required

[68] The World Bank, 'Sovereign ESG Data Framework', https://esgdata.worldbank.org/data/framework?lang=en, accessed 12 August 2023.

[69] Koh, Jerry K.C., and Leong, Victoria, 'The Rise of the Sustainability Reporting Megatrend: A Corporate Governance Perspective' (2017) 18 *Business Law International*, 233, 237.

[70] European Commission, 'Corporate Sustainability Reporting', https://finance.ec.europa.eu/capital-markets-union-and-financial-markets/company-reporting-and-auditing/company-reporting/corporate-sustainability-reporting_en, accessed 12 August 2023.

[71] Directive 2014/95/EU of the European Parliament and of the Council of 22 October 2014 amending Directive 2013/34/EU as regards disclosure of non-financial and diversity information by certain large undertakings and groups (OJ L 330, 15 November 2014, pp 1–9).

to disclose. It became active in January 2023 and will be gradually implemented over the next five years. Around 49,000 firms, mainly including major multinational corporations, are projected to come under the scope of these regulations. The updated regulations will guarantee that investors and stakeholders obtain necessary data to evaluate companies' societal and environmental influence, along with assessing financial implications stemming from climate change and sustainability matters. The initial implementation of these regulations is set for the 2024 financial year, with companies expected to adhere to them for reports released in 2025.[72]

The US, home to many major energy companies, has not been overly active in the area. The US Securities and Exchange Commission (SEC) has published its proposal for a climate risk disclosure rule in March 2022 and expected to be finalized around October 2023.[73] The proposed rules would mandate companies to incorporate specific climate-related details into their registration statements and regular reports. This includes information about climate-related risks that could notably affect their business, financial condition, or operational outcomes. Additionally, certain climate-related financial metrics would be required within a note to their audited financial statements. This necessary climate-related risk information would encompass the disclosure of a company's greenhouse gas emissions, a widely used measure for evaluating exposure to such risks.[74]

ESG disclosure requirements and the absence of clear rules, for many years, have led to legal disputes, as seen in the ExxonMobil case. The New York state attorney general's office's investigations, based on the New York anti-fraud law 'Martin Act', against ExxonMobil led to a case against the company. The key claim was that ExxonMobil misled investors by fraudulently employing two sets of books to calculate profits and losses on investments and the risks it faced as governments act to

[72] European Commission, 'Corporate Sustainability Reporting' (n. 83).

[73] The US Exchange and Securities and Exchange Commission, 'The Enhancement and Standardization of Climate-Related Disclosures for Investors' (2022), https://www.sec.gov/files/rules/proposed/2022/33-11042.pdf, accessed 12 August 2023.

[74] The US Exchange and Securities and Exchange Commission, 'Enhancement and Standardization of Climate-Related Disclosures Fact Sheet' (2022), https://www.sec.gov/files/33-11042-fact-sheet.pdf, accessed 12 August 2023.

reduce greenhouse gas emissions.[75] ExxonMobil received a favourable judgment from the New York Supreme Court, which ruled that the New York AG couldn't prove any investor had been misled. This is significant because the AG didn't meet the requirements of the Martin Act, which doesn't necessitate proving fraudulent intent (unlike federal securities laws). The AG also opted not to challenge the ruling on appeal. Despite this outcome, such cases are becoming more common, underscoring the growing ESG risks in the energy sector. Further, energy companies encounter challenges with ESG disclosure requirements, notably the ambiguity around shareholder resolutions. These resolutions may appear to request ESG transparency, but often aim to restrict a company's decisions and its directors' freedom.

Finally, companies are facing escalating pressure to genuinely uphold sustainability pledges to avoid the increasing wave of greenwashing allegations from environmental groups and investors. Legal challenges concerning greenwashing are mounting, both in courts and at the SEC, with advocates and investors targeting alleged misleading portrayals of corporate environmental and climate commitments. Environmental, social, and governance (ESG) matters are becoming a significant aspect of this legal trend. Shell Plc recently (February 2023) faced claims of distorting its renewable energy investment statements, with a filing under scrutiny by the SEC's Climate and ESG Task Force; the company maintains its full compliance with SEC and reporting requirements.[76]

2.3.6 *Insurance Risks in the Energy Transition*

Amidst the escalating climate crisis, acquiring insurance for energy projects has become notably challenging. According to the *Insure Our Future* website[77] 45 companies have committed to end or restrict underwriting for coal projects, this number for tar sands and oil and gas projects

[75] Natalie Nowiski, 'Rising Above the Storm: Climate Risk Disclosure and Its Current and Future Relevance to the Energy Sector' (2018) 39(1) *Energy Law Journal*, 27.

[76] Jennifer Hijazi, 'Shell Greenwashing Challenge Highlights Risk of ESG Claims' (Blomberg Law 2023) https://news.bloomberglaw.com/environment-and-energy/shell-greenwashing-challenge-highlights-risk-of-esg-claims, accessed 13 August 2023.

[77] Insure Our Future, is a global campaign of NGOs and social movements that hold the insurance industry accountable for its role in the climate crisis.

are 25 and 17 respectively.[78] This will set in motion a chain reaction, resulting in a higher frequency of instances where the state, acting as the insurer of last resort, will need to assume a more active role. Consequently, this dynamic will prompt the public to intensify their scrutiny of the overall merits of fossil fuel development and its continuity. One pivotal aspect concerning insurance pertains to forthcoming risks. The unease among investors is evident, underscored by a recent communication from a substantial and influential consortium of investors to the US Federal Reserve System. This letter delineated the risks emanating from climate change, underscored the urgency of prompt action, and underscored the pivotal role of the financial regulator in addressing these concerns.[79]

In June 2021, the Net-Zero Insurance Alliance (NZIA) was established with the goal of harnessing the substantial influence and resources of the insurance industry to facilitate the global shift towards a low-carbon economy.[80] Convened by the UN Environment Programme (UNEP), the alliance garnered 29 insurers and reinsurers from 13 countries at its peak, collectively representing more than $700 billion, which is over 14% of global written premiums.[81] Nevertheless, despite its initial success, the alliance has encountered mounting political opposition from certain Republicans in the United States. These individuals contend that the cooperative endeavours to diminish clients' carbon emissions could potentially infringe upon antitrust regulations. Consequently, this resistance has triggered a wave of departures, resulting in the current membership tally of 11 companies.[82]

[78] Insure Our Future, 'Number of Companies with Fossil Fuel Exclusion Policies, by Sector' (2023), https://global.insure-our-future.com/, accessed 13 August 2023.

[79] Ceres, 'Letter to the US Federal Reserve System' (21 July 2020), www.ceres.org/sites/default/files/, Federal%20Regulators%20Letter.pdf, accessed 20 December 2020.

[80] UNEP, 'World-Leading Insurers and United Nations Launch Pioneering Target-Setting Protocol to Accelerate Transition to Net-Zero Economy' (2023), https://www.unepfi.org/industries/insurance/launch-of-nzia-target-setting-protocol-version-1-0/, accessed 14 August 2023.

[81] Glasgow Financial Alliance for Net Zero, '2022 Progress Report' (2022), https://assets.bbhub.io/company/sites/63/2022/10/GFANZ-2022-Progress-Report.pdf, accessed 14 August 2023.

[82] Wilkes, Tommy, Hübner Alexander, and Sims, Tom, 'Insurers Flee Climate Alliance After ESG Backlash in the U.S.' (Rutters, 26 May 2023), https://www.reuters.com/business/allianz-decides-leave-net-zero-insurance-alliance-2023-05-25/, accessed 14 August 2023.

In spite of the ongoing departure of NZIA members, which has raised doubts about the alliance's future, even ex-NZIA members continue to uphold their individual sustainability commitments. Generally, the global insurance industry is beginning to increase the price of insurance for coal projects or simply state they will not insure such projects. Part of the challenge globally is the over-reliance on and technology lock-in to conventional energy sources. There is a new challenge as well in more affordable low-carbon energy that also meets national energy and climate goals. There is a need for investment decisions to move towards a more long-term focus, and this is expressed as a key issue by the actuarial profession in terms of managing risk regarding climate change.[83] In a similar way, a leading McKinsey report highlights that the lack of diversification in energy strategies by many companies and countries is a problem, and that these stakeholders need to realise opportunities from decarbonization, which are less risky,[84] and in part due to current or anticipated future lack of availability of insurance.

Insurance risk is a justice risk that is fast emerging. It takes into account several of the other justice risks and will result in increased application of justice in energy decision-making. The capture of risk data is highlighting the exposure of conventional energy sources to climate risk that results in increasing insurance costs and, therefore, increasing borrowing costs. This is in part why early in 2020, the BlackRock Chairman and Chief Executive Officer stated, in his annual address to shareholders, that there will be a major reallocation of capital towards sustainable investments that will be driven by climate risk—and this is an important statement by a firm that manages nearly $7 trillion in assets.[85] And indeed, it is also significant

[83] Institute and Faculty of Actuaries, 'Climate Change: Managing Risk and Uncertainty: Policy Briefing' (2015), www.actuaries.org.uk/system/files/field/document/Climate%20Change%20Managing%20Risk%20and%20Uncertainty%20-%20Policy%20Brief.pdf, accessed 20 December 2020.

[84] McKinsey Global Institute, 'Climate Risk and Response: Physical Hazards and Socioeconomic Impacts' (16 January 2020), www.mckinsey.com/business-functions/sustainability/our-insights/climate-risk-and-response-physical-hazards-and-socioeconomic-impacts#, accessed 20 December 2020.

[85] Marketwatch, (R Koning Beal), 'BlackRock's Fink Pressed to Take Action over Words in Dumping Fossil Fuels' (15 January 2020), www.marketwatch.com/story/blackrocks-fink-pressed-for-action-over-words-in-dumping-fossil-fuels-2020-01-14?mod=article_inline, accessed 20 December 2020.

in this context that BP would later write off £17.5 billion in assets from their balance sheet.[86]

2.3.7 Risk of Environmental Risk Assessments

The Environmental Impact Assessment (EIA), which stands as one of the most widely utilized tools in environmental management, has primarily concentrated on the evaluation of the environmental and social impacts of a project. However, only recently has it truly started to contribute to the development of a low-carbon economy. The EIA ensures that environmental concerns are considered from the very beginning of new projects, or their changes or extensions.[87] This paper does not seek to extensively delve into the details of EIAs,[88] but its main objective is to centre on the influence of EIAs on energy project development and creating risk for those projects.

As depicted Environmental Impact Assessments (EIAs) are engaged right from the beginning of the project life cycle, at the planning phase, and impact on the project risk immediately—hence their importance. Fundamentally, the process of EIA relates to procedural justice on three levels: —international, national and local:

- International: in securing finance for the project this will require an EIA to be produced for the financing institution under international banking standards – the Equator principles (this may be different for a company who will finance the project in-house or a national company who avails of financing options within the country

[86] BP to Take up to $17.5bn Hit on Assets After Cutting Energy Price Outlook. *Financial Times*, 15 June 2020, www.ft.com/content/2d84fc23-f38d-498f-9065-598f47e1ea09, accessed 20 December 2020.

[87] European Commission, 'Environmental Impact Assessment'. https://environment.ec.europa.eu/law-and-governance/environmental-assessments/environmental-impact-assessment_en, accessed 20 August 2023.

[88] The literature on EIAs is extensive from a legal and also an interdisciplinary perspective. There is research written on all aspects of the EIA process, and more can be found in the journal Environmental Impact Assessment Review. EIAs are the cause of many legal cases each year all over the world. A very comprehensive book on the subject matter is Environmental Impact Assessment by Tromans, although it has a UK focus; and it contains a very good approach from an EU law perspective: S Tromans, Environmental Impact Assessment (2nd edn, Bloomsbury Professional Ltd., 2012).

but the likelihood is there would remain some environmental impact statement produced);

- National: Has to adhere to national EIA legislation and submit an Environmental Impact Statement (EIS) which has to be approved before the project receives permission to start; and
- Local: The EIA process has to include several elements of public participation and involve these local stakeholders in the plans for the development of the project'.[89]

There also is an additional justice perspective, from a global point of view, where the EIA process has to be seen as a success as it has in essence promoted the philosophical ideal that people are all world citizens—i.e., cosmopolitan justice.[90] This will be discussed further in the context of two cases in 2019, in Australia and Kenya.

The regulations concerning Environmental Impact Assessments (EIAs) have undergone periodic modifications both on a national and global scale since their inception. Especially within the past decade, these changes have led to additional requirements, including the need to (1) showcase a heightened level of independence in the process, (2) collect and employ a greater amount of data, (3) analyse the combined effects of the project along with pre-existing projects in the vicinity, and (4) demonstrate a deliberate exploration of alternatives (alternative projects).

The significance of effectiveness in decision-making has amplified within the realms of environmental impact assessment (EIA) research.[91] This is evidenced by the increased stringency of EIA application at national and international levels, including instances such as international banking rules (known as the Equator Principles) now make the EIA a

[89] Heffron, R.J., 'The Role of Justice in Developing Critical Minerals' (2020) 7(3) *The Extractives Industry and Society*, 855.

[90] Cosmopolitan philosophy is the belief that we are all 'world citizens'. Cosmopolitanism has existed in some form since the ancient Greeks. The first philosopher in the West to give a perfectly explicit expression of cosmopolitanism was the Socratically-inspired Cynic Diogenes in the fourth century BC—it is said that when asked where he came from, he replied 'I am a citizen of the world' (Diogenes Laertius VI 63): Stanford Encyclopaedia of Philosophy, 2013 (Revised), 'Cosmopolitanism' http://plato.stanford.edu, accessed 20 December 2020.

[91] Caro-Gonzalez, Ana L., and others, 'From Procedural to Transformative: A Review of the Evolution of Effectiveness in EIA' (2023) 103 *Environmental Impact Assessment Review*, 107256.

prerequisite for project financing. Further, year-on-year the amount of data required in EIAs is increasing, with more data collection on the socio-economic impacts of an energy project (such as will be highlighted below in relation to the case law).

At present, the Equator Principles, which have been embraced by 138 financial institutions across 38 nations globally, are the established guidelines for banks and investors to address potential social and environmental impacts of significant projects that require funding. These principles have gained prominence since their inception in 2003. Since 2003, BankTrack has served as a monitor for the Equator Principles and their application. It has assessed projects funded under the Equator Principles to gauge their adherence, as well as evaluated Equator Principles implementation aspects like reporting, transparency, and project-related grievance processes.[92] International banks are now linking non-compliance with these principles to higher project risks, leading them to withdraw their support for such endeavors. In this context, what is originally regarded as international 'soft' law essentially transforms into 'hard' law.

It should be noted that there is additional support for EIA legislation at the international level, through an international agreement called the Aarhus Convention 1998—known as the Convention on Access to Information, Public Participation in Decision-Making and Access to Justice in Environmental Matters. This agreement allows for public participation in energy projects, and public access to environmental data, and is an agreement signed by 39 countries but with 47 parties to it. The result is that there is added enforcement to national EIA legislation, but this was a convention advanced by the United Nations Economic Commission for Europe (UN ECE) so is limited mostly to the EU and neighbouring countries.

Two recent cases on EIAs demonstrate the new risk associated with the EIA, and its vital role in project development. The interesting issue here too is that one example is from the developed world and one from the developing world, which highlights that the EIA is bringing in change. The EIA demonstrates that the collection and utilisation of data are now changing the nature of what energy projects can be built by virtue of a failure by certain projects to make it through the EIA process; and this is expected to rise. Recent decision-making in the legal courts after

[92] Bancktrack, 'Tracking the Equator Principles', https://www.banktrack.org/campaign/tracking_the_equator_principles, accessed 20 August 2023.

EIAs were challenged, in particular in Australia and Kenya, demonstrated that the data on socio-economic benefits and other costings have proved inadequate and/or over-/under-estimated. Groups opposed to particular energy projects are increasingly able to obtain data that challenges that of the project developer.

In 2019, two coal projects were stopped, one in Australia and one in Kenya, because their EIAs were considered unsatisfactory. The key reasons for the failure were that the EIAs lacked completeness in terms of data provision, the poor assessment of the social and environmental impacts from the existing data, and that the projects' positive economic contributions were overestimated.[93] The amount of data that must be presented in the EIA process is growing, and the link between EIAs, data and justice has already been identified.[94] These latter two cases and others highlight the rise of data, and data that is accessible, and they demonstrate how recent changes in EIA legislation around the world have risen to prominence and are again increasing the risk profile of energy projects.

2.3.8 The Risk from Climate Change Action

Climate change has often been described as 'the challenge of our generation', with broad international consensus on the need to limit global temperature increases to 1.5 °C above pre-industrial levels to reduce the risks and impacts of climate change, such as increase in sea level, high temperatures, spread of disease and etc. Indeed, 189 of the 195 signatories to the 2015 Paris Agreement on Climate Change have now ratified the treaty.[95]

Climate change litigation is increasingly being used as a tool to recover 'the costs of climate-related damage and adaptation, but also as a means to

[93] Nogrady, B., 'Landmark Australian Ruling Rejects Coal Mine Over Global Warming' (11 February 2019) *Nature*, www.nature.com/articles/d41586-019-00545-8, accessed 20 December 2020; Herbling, D., *Kenya Cancels Environment License of $2 Billion Coal-Power Plant*. Bloomberg, 26 June 2019, www.bloomberg.com/news/articles/2019-06-26/kenya-cancels-environment-license-of-2-billion-coal-power-plant, accessed 20 December 2020.

[94] Sherren, K., and others, 'Digital Archives, Big Data and Image-Based Culturomics for Social Impact Assessment: Opportunities and Challenges' (2017) 67 *Environmental Impact Assessment Review*, 23.

[95] https://treaties.un.org/Pages/ViewDetails.aspx?src=IND&mtdsg_no=XXVII-7-d&chapter=27&clang=_en.

promote and accelerate policy change and the transition towards a lower global carbon economy'[96]—and this cost recovery can be described as an element of restorative justice. The recent report from the UN Environment Programme (UNEP) and the Sabin Center for Climate Change Law indicates that the count of climate change court cases has more than doubled since 2017.[97]

In addition, in October 2021, HRC adopted a historic resolution (A/HRC/RES/48/13) recognizing the human right to a clean, healthy and sustainable environment. As a result, one of the considerable issues in the climate change cases is related to climate rights, including the rights to life, health, food, water, liberty, family life, a healthy environment, a safe climate. As of 31 December 2023, 2180 climate change litigation cases in at least 65 different countries had been reported globally. The vast majority of these cases (1522) were brought in the United States, with growing jurisprudence in other highly developed countries, including Australia, the United Kingdom and Germany respectively.[98] Cases have also been brought in the International Court of Justice, within the European Union courts, before the Inter-American Commission on Human Rights and before numerous UN committees. A more recent development has been the trend towards cases being brought in developing countries, including India, Pakistan, Uganda, Colombia and the Philippines.[99]

Governments are most commonly sued in non-US cases, with the case law showing that decisions relating to environmental assessment of

[96] Clarke, Mark, and Daley, Katherine, Climate Change Litigation Is Driving the Transition, *Petroleum Economist*, 27 January 2020, www.petroleum-economist.com/articles/low-carbon-energy/energy-transition/2020/climate-change-litigation-is-driving-the-transition, accessed 20 December 2020.

[97] UNEP, 'Global Climate Litigation Report: 2023 Status Review' (2023), https://www.unep.org/resources/report/global-climate-litigation-report-2023-status-review, accessed 20 August 2023.

[98] UN, 'Global Climate Litigation Report: 2023 Status Review', https://wedocs.unep.org/bitstream/handle/20.500.11822/43008/global_climate_litigation_report_2023.pdf?sequence=3, accessed 20 August 2023.

[99] Setzer, Joana and Byrnes, Rebecca, *Global Trends in Climate Change Litigation: 2019 Snapshot* (Grantham Research Institute on Climate Change and the Environment and the Centre for Climate Change Economics and Policy, July 2019), www.lse.ac.uk/GranthamInstitute/wp-content/uploads/2019/07/GRI_Global-trends-in-climate-change-litigation-2019-snapshot-2.pdf, accessed 20 December 2020.

projects and permitting of developments, greenhouse gas reductions and trading and human rights are most likely to be challenged in the courts. For example, in *Urgenda Foundation v. State of the Netherlands*,[100] the Urgenda Foundation successfully used a combination of tort law and international law to argue that the Dutch government had breached its duty of care to the Dutch people, under Articles 2 and 8 of the European Convention on Human Rights, in failing to take sufficient actions to mitigate and prevent climate change.[101] This decision was upheld in Court of Appeal of the Hague, with the court finding that the Dutch government was required to adopt stricter emissions reductions targets, reducing emissions by at least 25% on 1990 levels by 2020.[102]

Between 2020 and 2022, there has been a noticeable rise in the occurrence of lawsuits involving non-government entities as private companies and financial institutions.[103] An increasing number of climate change cases are being brought in the energy sector against private corporations seeking to (i) hold them responsible for climate change damage resulting from their projects; (ii) force them to incorporate climate risk into their investment decisions; and (iii) disclose climate risks to their shareholders.[104] It is this kind of climate change litigation that can expose *justice risks* by shifting away from a narrow, purely project-level focus to legal interventions that hold corporations directly to account for the climate consequences of their actions through novel forms of litigation.[105]

As an example, in the case of *Milieudefensie* et al. *v. Royal Dutch Shell* (2022) the District Court of The Hague ruled that Royal Dutch Shell, a multinational oil and gas company based in the Netherlands, must

[100] [2015] HAZA C/09/00456689. See also Heffron, R.J., 'State of the Netherlands v Urgenda (Case Note)' (2020) 1(1) *Global Energy Law & Sustainability*, 104.

[101] Setzer and Byrnes (n. 81).

[102] Corbel, Andrew, A New Era of Climate Change Litigation in Australia? *Corrs Chambers Westgarth*, 8 April 2019, https://corrs.com.au/insights/a-new-era-of-climate-change-litigation-in-australia, accessed 20 December 2020.

[103] UN, 'Global Climate Litigation Report: 2023 Status Review', https://wedocs.unep.org/bitstream/handle/20.500.11822/43008/global_climate_litigation_report_2023.pdf?sequence=3, accessed 20 August 2023.

[104] Setzer and Byrnes (n. 81) 8–9.

[105] Peel, Jacqueline, Osofsky, Hari, and Foerster, Anita, 'Shaping the 'Next Generation' of Climate Change Litigation in Australia' (2017) *MelbULawRw*, 39.

decrease CO_2 emissions linked to its products by 45% compared to 2019 levels by the year 2030. This ruling marks the inaugural occurrence of a private corporation being mandated to adhere to the Paris Agreement's guidelines and being recognized as having an obligation to mitigate GHG emissions according to the Paris Agreement.

Governments, private corporations and investors must consider the climate impacts of projects in their decision-making during both the due diligence phase and the environmental assessment and approvals process. Once approved, proactive steps need to be taken to mitigate or prevent climate damage, and the exposure of companies to climate risks should be disclosed to shareholders—they should be future-proofing their decision-making.[106] Importantly, many of these risks need to be assessed on a cumulative basis, meaning that the importance of climate change litigation will only continue to grow in the coming years.

2.3.9 Risk from the Rules of Foreign Investment

The idea that foreign investment is intrinsically positive and should remain untouched has been a prevailing concept in recent decades. This has consequently resulted in excessive protection for energy investors, weakening the institutions responsible for monitoring their effects on society and the environment.[107] Nevertheless, as concerns grow over the damage inflicted on nature and people—such as air and land pollution, which disproportionately affect indigenous communities, this prevailing belief is facing increasing challenges.[108]

Recent cases in countries like Bolivia, Kenya, and Peru highlight key legal issues such as the importance of EIAs, social licences to operate, and energy finance reserve obligations, as well as energy justice issues. An ongoing case in Nigeria between the Nigerian government and a foreign investor, with an award worth approximately $9.6 billion at stake, will be

[106] Add reference.

[107] Heffron, Raphael J., and others, 'Pathways of Scholarship for Energy Justice and the Social Contract' (2023) 41(2) *Journal of Energy & Natural Resources Law*, 211–232.

[108] Droubi, S., Elizondo, C.J.F., and Heffron, R.J., 'Latin America, Indigenous Peoples and Investments: Resistance and Accommodation' in Droubi, S., and Elizondo, C.J.F. (eds) *Latin America and International Investment Law: A Mosaic of Resistance* (Manchester UP, 2022).

transformative on several issues.[109] The first question is whether foreign investments should receive full protection, and the second question then arises whether an energy arbitration case should be subject to advances in public policymaking.

The answer should be a resounding 'yes', especially as an energy case involves energy, environmental, and climate change issues and generally also includes closely related issues such as international development, finance, and taxation. The UK High Court stated in August 2019 that there was no public policy issue. As governments intensify efforts to reduce reliance on fossil fuels, energy companies dealing with oil, gas, and coal might exploit investment law to protect themselves from the costs of the energy transition or to hinder the transition altogether. Investor-State dispute settlement (ISDS) claims under agreements like the Energy Charter Treaty (ECT) enable foreign investors to file compensation lawsuits against a State through confidential arbitration if their profits are negatively impacted by regulations or State actions.[110] The ECT has been cited in 17 *percent* of all ISDS cases involving fossil fuels, making it the most frequently utilized international investment agreement in such cases.[111]

Further, during 2021, major energy companies RWE and Uniper initiated ISDS procedures using the Energy Charter Treaty (ECT) against the Netherlands, challenging the Dutch government's plan to phase out coal power plants by 2030. Although Uniper recently dropped its claim against the Netherlands as part of a bailout agreement with the German government, the RWE case remains unresolved.[112] In July 2023, the European Commission has suggested that the EU, its Member States, and Euratom

[109] For background, see (1) Reuters (2020), www.reuters.com/article/us-nigeria-arbitration/nigerian-court-orders-firm-that-won-9-billion-case-against-government-to-forfeit-assets-idUSKBN1W42IG, accessed 20 December 2020; and (2) Heffron, R.J., and Bausch, R., 'Process & Industrial Developments Limited v The Federal Republic of Nigeria (Case Note)' (2020) 1(1) *Global Energy Law & Sustainability*, 101.

[110] Centre for International Environmental Law, 'Investors v. Climate Action' (2022), https://www.ciel.org/wp-content/uploads/2023/02/CIEL_blog_Investors-v.-Climate-Action_Sept-2022.pdf, accessed 20 August 2023.

[111] Di Salvatore, Lea, 'Investor–State Disputes in the Fossil Fuel Industry (IISD 2022)', https://www.iisd.org/system/files/2022-01/investor%E2%80%93state-disputes-fossil-fuel-industry.pdf, accessed 20 August 2023.

[112] Climate Case Chart, 'Uniper v. the Netherlands', https://climatecasechart.com/non-us-case/uniper-v-netherlands/, accessed 20 August 2023.

jointly exit the Energy Charter Treaty, mainly because the treaty is no longer compatible with the EU's enhanced climate ambition under the European Green Deal and the Paris Agreement.[113]

If the energy transition is to happen, rules around investor protection will have to recognise the transition and its foreseeability—again the idea of 'future-proofing' mentioned in the previous section. This controversial issue of the rules of foreign investment in this respect is the role and responsibility of governments in soliciting certain type of investments into their respective countries and energy mixes, and the role and responsibility of private undertakings making the investments. This will be an area of transformation over the next decade and will put significant risk on energy projects.

2.3.10 *The 2015 Paris Agreement 'Risk'*

On 12 December 2015, meeting in Paris under the auspices of the UN Framework Convention on Climate Change, 195 nations signed what has been hailed as an historic climate agreement. The agreement was recognised as a '*turning point, that this is the moment we finally determined we would save our planet*' and that the assembled nations '*share a sense of urgency about this challenge and a growing realization that it is within our power to do something about it*'.[114] The signatories pledged to reduce carbon emissions with the intent of keeping global warming below 2 °C while pursuing the more ambitious target of limiting temperature increases to 1.5 °C from pre-industrial levels. The actual commercial costs of implementing the Paris Agreement are difficult, if not impossible, to determine because the issue is susceptible to political polemics. In fact, the implementation of the agreement requires economic and social transformation of each country, which is really has only being realized over the last few years. Hence, that is why it poses as a significant and influential transition risk.

[113] European Commission, 'European Commission Proposes a Coordinated EU Withdrawal from the Energy Charter Treaty', https://energy.ec.europa.eu/news/european-commission-proposes-coordinated-eu-withdrawal-energy-charter-treaty-2023-07-07_en, accessed 20 August 2023.

[114] White House, 'Remarks by President Obama at the First Session of COP_{21}' (30 November 2015), www.whitehouse.gov/the-press-office/2015/11/30/remarks-president-obama-first-session-cop21; Coral Davenport, Nations Approve Landmark Climate Accord in Paris. *NY Times*, 12 December 2015, accessed 20 December 2020.

Although the short (11-page) agreement does not set legally binding emissions limits, the parties committed themselves to a regime that requires them to report on the progress of their commitments every five years. Since 2020, countries have been presenting their individual climate action blueprints, referred to as nationally determined contributions (NDCs). At five-year intervals, countries are expected to evaluate their advancements in enacting the accord via a procedure termed the global stocktake, with the initial one scheduled for 2023.[115] The NDCs are accompanied by international norms to ensure transparency and accountability. The NDCs are determined by each signatory rather than negotiated internationally. Notably, NDCs are required of all signatories rather than a selected and limited group of developed nations. Although not legally binding, they are subject to publicity. They are recorded in a public registry that is available for public dissemination, and to date over 180 states have registered their NDCs.[116]

In addition to the widespread adoption and commitment to addressing climate change, the agreement, importantly, contains a human rights provision. Although it was not included as an operative article, it was included in the preamble. The human rights language directs participants to consider their environmental obligations regarding human rights, including the right to health, the rights of indigenous peoples, the rights of immigrant children, and the rights of other vulnerable populations.[117] In this regard, the Supreme Court of Brazil has achieved a historic milestone by being the world's inaugural judicial body to acknowledge the Paris Agreement as a treaty safeguarding human rights. This decision carries substantial ramifications for both domestic and global legal frameworks. The ruling said "*Treaties on environmental law are a type of human*

[115] Lindsay Maizland, 'Global Climate Agreement: Successes and Failures (Council on Foreign Relations, 4 November 2022)', https://www.cfr.org/backgrounder/paris-global-climate-change-agreements#:~:text=Experts%20say%20the%20Paris%20Agreement,as%20heat%20waves%20and%20floods, accessed 20 August 2023.

[116] Bodansky, Daniel, 'The Paris Climate Agreement: A New Hope?' (2016) 110 *American Journal of International Law*, 288.

[117] Carlene, Cinnamon and Colevecchio, J.D., 'Balancing Equity and Effectiveness: The Paris Agreement & the Future of International Climate Change Law' (2019) 27 *New York University Environmental Law Journal*, 107.

rights treaty and, for that reason, enjoy supranational status".[118] Further work on human rights also highlights this as a significant risk in the energy transition that corporations and governments need to adhere to.[119]

2.3.11 *The Risk from the Rise of Imagery and Data*

Climate change commitments are meaningless without a coordinated collective response, a task made complex by the fact that climate change appears intangible to numerous individuals, doesn't follow a straightforward path, demands global collaboration, and has turned into a deeply politicized issue. Considering these difficulties, it's not surprising that that effectively communicating the issue of climate change—and getting people to care about it—continues to be a complex task for various groups, particularly those aiming to synchronize public awareness of climate change with the scientific consensus.[120] Imagery and data have emerged as important tools for conveying information about climate change, and project development and increasing the risks that need to be managed by energy stakeholders.

Both are now having an impact and increasing the risk profile of energy projects. These are also both areas of research growth as, particularly in law, both are utilised in and are valuable sources of evidence in legal courtrooms and prior legal proceedings. For example, personal technology is having a big impact in terms of using imagery to change public policy; and it should be noted that images already play a role in both criminal and civil legal systems. The difference now, however, is that personal technology has caused images to be accessible to all and to be captured by all. That this should spread into mainstream society in terms of the effects of climate change should be no surprise, but it is having a major effect. Key issues around personal decisions on where to live, lifestyle, and tourism

[118] Kaminski, Isabella, 'Brazilian Court World's First to Recognise Paris Agreement as Human Tights Treaty' (7 July 2022), https://www.climatechangenews.com/2022/07/07/brazilian-court-worlds-first-to-recognise-paris-agreement-as-human-rights-treaty/, accessed 20 August 2023.

[119] Add reference here.

[120] Mooseder, Angelina, and others, '(Social) Media Logics and Visualizing Climate Change: 10 Years of #climatechange Images on Twitter' (2023) 9(1) *Social Media+ Society* https://doi.org/10.1177/20563051231164310.

will change, and are already influencing societal development. The literature is growing in this area alongside the realisation of the effects of this imagery.[121]

The literature on imagery to date has concerned mainly communication and engagement practices[122]; however, it is proposed here that the role of imagery has become more powerful. There are some who argue that in processes such as an EIA process, images are 'made to fit' the reality they are intended to serve.[123] But local communities are increasingly utilising technology to hold energy companies accountable, and this is changing the behaviour of the energy companies who must ensure that what they do in one part of the world does not impact their business in another part of the world. Local communities can share and transmit images that become available to other local communities worldwide.

Data is also becoming more readily accessible, and this is informing and influencing behaviour. For example, the use of data is becoming influential in courtrooms. There will be an impact, then, on the risk profile of a project as the project developer's data comes under increased scrutiny. However, data can also play a powerful role in a positive way and thus, for some projects, it will reduce the risk as it shows the benefits of such technology. For example, increasingly data is used to ensure more flexibility is utilised in the electricity system.[124]

The intermittent nature of renewables calls for grid stability solutions. The industry is moving from commodity-based to technology-driven markets for renewable integration. Artificial intelligence (AI) is pivotal in this transition, enhancing prediction, demand forecasting, and operational efficiency. Alongside technologies like the internet of things (IoT), sensors, and big data, AI unlocks renewable potential. Failing to adopt AI risks lagging behind. Given the complexity of energy grids, AI's speed

[121] O'Neill, S.J., and Smith, N., 'Climate Change and Visual Imagery' (2014) 5 *WIREs Climate Change*, 73.

[122] O'Neill, S.J., and others, 'On the Use of Imagery for Climate Change Engagement' (2013) 23(2) *Global Environmental Change*, 413.

[123] De Oliveira, A. Roque, and Partidario, M., 'You See What I Mean?—A Review of Visual Tools for Inclusive Public Participation in EIA Decision-Making Processes' (2020) 83 *Environmental Impact Assessment Review*, 106413.

[124] Heffron, R., and others, 'Industrial Demandside Flexibility: A Key Element of a Just Energy Transition and Industrial Development' (2020) 269(115026) *Applied Energy*, https://doi.org/10.1016/j.apenergy.2020.115026.

and accuracy make it a suitable choice. As we enter the Fourth Industrial Revolution, AI stands as a key tool in achieving renewable energy success.[125]

2.3.12 *The Risk from the United Nations Sustainable Development Goals*

The SDGs were unanimously adopted by 193 UN member states on 25 September 2015 as part of UN Resolution 70/1, 'Transforming Our World: the 2030 Agenda for Sustainable Development'.[126] The SDGs were designed to follow on from the Millennium Development Goals and established the post-2015 global development agenda until 2030. They comprise 17 goals, with an associated 169 targets and 232 indicators, which are used to measure performance.

The SDGs are wide-ranging in their design, providing a clear link between sustainable development and the international human rights agenda. As a result, the SDGs have been described as 'integrated and indivisible'.[127] Despite this, there has been broad acknowledgement of the critical role that the energy transition will play in achieving the SDGs, with SDG 7—to 'ensure access to affordable, reliable, sustainable and modern energy for all'—often described as a key enabler for all of the other SDGs.[128] This reflects the interlinkages between energy and poverty eradication (SDG 1); reduction of inequalities (SDG 10); gender equality (SDG 5); jobs (SDG 8); climate change (SDG 13); food security (SDG 2); heath (SDG 3); education (SDG 4); clean water and sanitation (SDG 6); sustainable cities and communities (SDG 11); innovation, transport,

[125] Warren, Ben, and de Giovanni, Arnaud, *Will Local Ambition Fast-Track or Frustrate the Global Energy Transition?* (EY, 2023), https://www.ey.com/en_gl/recai/will-local-ambition-fast-track-or-frustrate-the-global-energy-transition, accessed 20 August 2023.

[126] Lobel, Nathan and others, 'Mapping the Renewable Energy Sector to the Sustainable Development Goals: An Atlas' (Columbia Center on Sustainable Investment, Equitable Origin, Business & Human Rights Resource Centre and the Sustainable Development Solutions Network, June 2019), 5.

[127] Ibid., 14.

[128] United Nations, *Analysis of the Voluntary National Reviews Relating to Sustainable Development Goal 7* (United Nations, 2018), https://sustainabledevelopment.un.org/content/documents/258321159DESASDG7_VNR_Analysis2018_final.pdf, accessed 20 December 2020.

and industrialisation (SDG 9); peace and security (SDG 16), refugees and other situations of displacement.[129]

Based on the latest Report (2023), there are 675 million people without access to electricity and 2.3 billion people without access to clean cooking facilities in 2021. While there has been progress compared to the statistics from 2010, which showed 1.1 billion people without access to electricity and 2.9 billion people without access to clean cooking,[130] the pace of progress is still too slow for the achievement of the 2030 goals.[131] This problem is compounded when the enabler role of SDG 7 in achieving the other SDGs is considered. To achieve SDG 7, investment in this area needs to more than double the $US500 billion per annum currently being spent, to $US 1.2 trillion per annum until 2030.[132] This financial commitment would encompass around $51 billion annually to ensure universal electricity access, approximately $4 billion for promoting clean cooking access, over $660 billion directed towards renewable energy initiatives, and an additional $600 billion dedicated to advancing energy-efficient technologies.[133]

A further impact of the SDGs is that they have brought human rights considerations within the energy sector into much starker focus, right down to the individual project level. This means that particularly for companies and financiers operating in this sector, the global expectations around their conduct are rapidly changing, impacting their exposure to legal and regulatory, reputational, financial, environmental and social risks.[134] In addition to companies being expected to comply with the UN Guiding Principles on Business and Human Rights, the International

[129] Lobel and others (n. 104).

[130] IEA, 'Tracking SDG7: The Energy Progress Report 2023', https://trackingsdg7.esmap.org/data/files/download-documents/sdg7-report2023-full_report.pdf, accessed 20 August 2023.

[131] Ibid.

[132] United Nations, *2018 HLPF Review of SDG Implementation: SDG 7—Ensure Access to Affordable, Reliable, Sustainable and Modern Energy for All* (United Nations, 2018), 4.

[133] IEA, 'Tracking SDG7: The Energy Progress Report 2019', https://trackingsdg7.esmap.org/data/files/download-documents/chapter_5_outlook_for_sdg7.pdf, accessed 20 August 2023.

[134] Ibid., 6.

Finance Corporation (IFC) Performance Standards, the OECD Guidelines for Multinational Enterprises, the International Labour Organsiation (ILO) Core Conventions, and the Equator Principles, good corporate citizens are now expected to model the impacts of the SDGs on their projects throughout their operational processes and supply chains, as well as on their corporate governance decisions.[135]

Companies that adopt this approach not only reduce their project risk by improving their social licence to operate but also are more attractive to investors, financiers and host governments by facilitating a just, equitable and inclusive framework for economic development. This enables companies to ensure that their operations do not increase transition (justice) risks for their host communities and the environment.[136]

[135] Ibid.

[136] Ibid., 16.

CHAPTER 3

Case Studies: Has the Energy Transition Impacted Extractive Contracts?

Abstract Effective extractive contract negotiations and having a competitive fiscal regime are essential for the proper governance of the extractive industries. By nature, the extractive industries which include oil, gas, coal and mining are finite resources. They are not only associated with various social impacts, but their impact on the environment cannot be ignored. There are several issues to be considered in order to ensure that the resources benefit the citizens of the country. These include among others good governance, transparency, availability of the necessary infrastructure, equity in the distribution of the revenues from the extractives, environmental protection to mention but a few. In addition to this, is the need to negotiate extractive contracts that benefit the relevant stakeholders including among others the host government, investors and the citizens. In this energy transition and climate change era, it becomes imperative to analyse whether the contracts that were negotiated after the 2015 Paris Agreement respond to the net-zero goals? This chapter, therefore, referring to different countries, will spotlight the key extractive contractual provisions that ought to be amended in order to align with the global net-zero goals.

V. R. Nalule et al., *Renegotiating Contracts for the Energy Transition in the Extractives Industry*, Just Transitions,
https://doi.org/10.1007/978-3-031-46258-0_3

Keywords Renegotiating extractive contracts · Energy transition · Climate change · Just transition · Energy justice · Extractives · Net zero · Extractive contracts · Fiscal regime · Stabilization clauses · Arbitration clauses

3.1 Introduction to Extractive Contracts and the Fiscal Regime

Effective extractive contract negotiations and having a competitive fiscal regime are essential for the proper governance of the extractive industries. By nature, the extractive industries which include oil, gas, coal and mining are finite resources.[1] They are not only associated with various social impacts, but their impact on the environment cannot be ignored.[2] Whereas several countries such as the Norway, Namibia, Botswana, the USA and many others have economically benefited from the development of their extractive industries, a few other countries like Nigeria have been categorised as examples of a resource curse.

There are several issues to be considered in order to ensure that the resources benefit the citizens of the country. These include among others good governance, transparency, availability of the necessary infrastructure, equity in the distribution of the revenues from the extractives, environmental protection to mention but a few.[3] In addition to this, is the need to negotiate extractive contracts that benefit the relevant stakeholders including among others the host government, investors and the citizens.[4] In this energy transition and climate change era, it becomes imperative to

[1] Nalule, V.R., and Babajide, N.A., 'Protecting Natural Gas Investments: Trends in Investment Treaties and Investors Projections in Africa' in *The Palgrave Handbook of Natural Gas and Global Energy Transitions* (Cham: Springer International Publishing, 2022 May 5), 461–481.

[2] Nalule, V.R., and Nalule, V.R,. 'Social and Environmental Impacts of Mining' (2020) *Mining and the Law in Africa: Exploring the Social and Environmental Impacts*, 51–81.

[3] Hilson, G., and Maconachie, R., '"Good Governance" and the Extractive Industries in Sub-Saharan Africa' (2008 December 29) 30(1) *Mineral Processing and Extractive Metallurgy Review*, 52–100.

[4] Nalule, V.R., (ed), *Mining Law and Governance in Africa: Transformation and Innovation for a Sustainable Mining Sector* (Taylor & Francis, 2023 June 9).

analyse whether the contracts that were negotiated after the 2015 Paris Agreement respond to the net-zero goals?

Besides the extractive contracts, the fiscal regimes should be competitive to respond to the net-zero goals and climate change targets. The fiscal regime is capable of supporting or constraining the energy transition initiatives and net-zero goals. Simply put, the fiscal regime refers to the set of instruments, laws, regulations, agreements or tools that stipulate how revenues from oil, gas and mining activities are to be shared between the State and the extractive companies (ECs).[5] Instability in the fiscal regimes has been experienced in different countries. These instabilities have not only been the main driver in negotiating extractive contracts and inclusion of certain provisions such as stabilisation clauses, but they have also influenced the enactment of new extractive laws. There are several questions that ought to be addressed regarding the fiscal regime. One may ask, what are the main drivers of unstable fiscal regimes? What would influence the host state to revise the fiscal terms to which it originally agreed with the investors? Dr. Carol Nakhle highlights the main drivers of fiscal regime instabilities as illustrated in the table below[6]:

As illustrated in Table 3.1, there are various factors that may influence instabilities in the fiscal regime. The same factors may also determine if the countries' fiscal regime is supporting or constraining the energy transition and net-zero goals. This section, therefore, referring to different countries, will spotlight the key extractive contractual provisions that ought to be amended in order to align with the global net-zero goals.

3.2 Extractives Laws and Their Transformation to Address Current Challenges

The extractive industries entails both fossil fuels and mining. As earlier discussed, the extractive industry is increasingly becoming essential for the energy transition. This is specifically true due to the crucial role of critical

[5] Olawuyi, D.S., *Extractives Industry Law in Africa* (Springer International Publishing, 2018 September 11).

[6] Mansour, M., and Nakhle, C., 'Fiscal Stabilization in Oil and Gas Contracts—Evidence and Implications', Oxford Institute for Energy Studies Paper: SP 37 (2016).

Table 3.1 Drivers of fiscal regime instabilities and changes

Factor	*Driver*
Oil prices	Typically, when the oil price is high, the government has the upper hand. Governments often change their fiscal terms to respond to oil prices
Investments	A significant rise in petroleum investments may encourage the host government to introduce a tax increase. However, an unexpected decline in investment may trigger the opposite response
Production life-cycle	Whereas governments are keen to attract investments before a discovery, by among other means, providing a favourable tax regime; often the same government will increase the taxes once commercial discoveries are made
Regional Trend and Neighbourhood Effect	A change in the fiscal regime of one country can influence neighbouring countries to do the same. This is so because most of the countries in the region are competing for the same few petroleum investors, so they endeavour to have similar tax policies
Changes in Political Conditions	Once a new government is ushered into the country, they often change the legal, regulatory and fiscal frameworks. As such, the petroleum fiscal regime designed by the previous administration will invariably be reviewed critically by a successor with a different political persuasion or ideology
Deteriorating Government Finances	When a country is going through an economic crisis, the government will take all measures to raise revenue, including increasing taxes for IOCs. In this respect, a country will make changes to the general fiscal regime, affecting not only the local industry and other sectors, but also the IOCs

Source Nakhle, 2016[7]; and Nalule, 2021[8]

[7] Mansour, M., and Nakhle, C., 'Fiscal Stabilization in Oil and Gas Contracts—Evidence and Implications', Oxford Institute for Energy Studies Paper: SP 37 (2016).

[8] Nalule, V.R., *Land Law and the Extractive Industries: Challenges and Opportunities in Africa* (Hart Publishers, 2021).

minerals which are required for the low-carbon technologies.[9] Important to note, however, is that the extractive industry does not only imply extraction of oil, gas, and other minerals from the earth's surface. Behind these activities are people, corporations, governments, and financial institutions that support the extraction of the resources.[10] The extractive laws and contracts therefore should reflect the interest of all these relevant stakeholders.

The international nature of extractive and energy resources implies that the governance and regulation of the industry is influenced by international law, regional law and national law. This is so, because of the capital-intensive nature of these projects and the international investments, as evidenced by the establishment of transboundary energy infrastructure such as oil and gas pipelines, oil refineries, and electricity transmission lines, just to mention but a few.[11]

Extractive and energy laws and policies have in the past been driven by the need to address pertinent challenges in our societies. In the nineteenth century for instance, most extractive and energy laws in the global north were focused on ensuring energy security. In Europe, this was illustrated by the crucial role of the Energy Charter Treaty. At the national level, countries focused on enhancing energy security by promoting the development of energy infrastructure. A case in point is the 2005 Energy Policy Act of the US, the main aim of which was to initiate several hundred billion dollars' worth of new energy infrastructure projects.[12] Similarly, the UK government declared that the goal of its Energy Act 2013 was to initiate £ 110 billion of new energy infrastructure.[13]

In the twenty-first century however, the global move to transition to a low-carbon economy has driven the enaction of energy laws that

[9] Acheampong, T., The Energy Transition and Critical Minerals in Ghana: Diversification Opportunities and Governance Challenges.

[10] Nalule, V.R., 'Modernisation of the Mining Laws and Key Issues for Consideration in Africa' (2023 June 9). *Mining Law and Governance in Africa: Transformation and Innovation for a Sustainable Mining Sector*.

[11] Cameron, P.D., and Stanley, M.C., *Oil, Gas, and Mining: A Sourcebook for Understanding the Extractive Industries* (World Bank Publications, 2017 June 1).

[12] Heffron, R.J., and Heffron, R.J., *What Is Energy Law?* (Springer International Publishing, 2021).

[13] Ibid.

promote renewable energy, energy efficiency and deployment of electric vehicles.[14] Besides the international 2015 Paris Agreement aimed at addressing climate change, different countries have gone ahead to enact national climate change laws. In extractive terms, the mining laws are now more focused on ensuring security of supply of the critical minerals.[15]

In the global south, the progressive nature of the extractive laws is visible in the various mining laws and legislations enacted. Basically, the mining sector is governed by various legislation, the key pieces being mining laws and regulations. Besides mining laws, other laws are relevant in the governance of the mining sector including environmental laws, taxation laws, land laws and employment laws.[16] On the African continent for instance, the progressive nature of mining laws is evidenced in the various mining codes. These codes are divided into different generations, including the first generation which comprises the mining legislation of the 1980s, the second generation which comprises mining legislation from the early to mid-1990s, and the third generation which refers to the mining legislation of the late 1990s.[17] The new wave of reforms in the current mining laws can arguably be referred to as the fourth generation of mining codes.

As illustrated by Dr. Victoria Nalule, the first generation of mining laws was characterised by the withdrawal of the state from actively being involved in the mining sector, as a way of attracting investors.[18] Ghana is a good example of this generation of laws. The second generation was characterised by the regulation of the mining sector, including putting into consideration environmental and health protection, which, contrary to present practice, were left to be a responsibility of the private sector,

[14] Nalule, V., and Acheampong, T., 'Energy Transition Indicators in African Countries: Managing the Possible Decline of Fossil Fuels and Tackling Energy Access Challenges' (2021 September 27) 12(1) *Journal of Sustainable Development Law and Policy (The)*, 1–48.

[15] Nalule, V.R., 'Justice in Managing the Nexus Between Mining, Energy Transitions, and Climate Change' in *Mining Law and Governance in Africa* (Routledge, 2023 June 9), 330–332.

[16] Nalule, V.R., and Nalule, V.R., 'Regulation of Mining in Africa' in *Mining and the Law in Africa: Exploring the Social and Environmental Impacts* (Palgrave, 2020), 19–50.

[17] Nalule, V.R., 'Modernisation of the Mining Laws and Key Issues for Consideration in Africa' in *Mining Law and Governance in Africa: Transformation and Innovation for a Sustainable Mining Sector* (Routledge, 2023 June 9).

[18] Ibid.

i.e., non-state actors.[19] Guinea provides a good example of this second-generation mining legislation. The late 1990s witnessed the emergence of the third generation of mining codes. Unlike the first generation, the third generation recognised and encouraged the role of the state in the facilitation and regulation of the mining sector, with the caveat that the reforms reduced the state' s role and ownership in the mining sector. Mali, Madagascar and Tanzania provide good examples of the third-generation laws.[20]

The discussion and examples in this section are clear indication that extractive laws have been transforming to address the current challenges in the industry. In the next section therefore, we shall ascertain whether extractive contracts have transformed to align with the net-zero goals.

3.3 Extractive Contracts: Are They Transforming to Align with Net-Zero Goals?

The discussion in this section will only focus on the key provisions in petroleum contracts. There are several petroleum agreements that a government must choose from. These include: a concession or licence agreement, a production-sharing agreement (PSA), a joint venture (JV) or a service agreement. These agreements govern the relationship between governments and oil investors. These are briefly discussed below.

As illustrated in Table 3.2, there different types of petroleum agreements. In the next section, we review the key provisions in these agreements to ascertain whether they align with the net-zero goals.

3.3.1 Case Studies: Contractual Provisions That Have an Impact on the Country's Alignment with the Net-Zero Goals

This section reviews and compares extractive contracts signed before the 2015 Paris Agreement, and those signed after 2015, to ascertain whether there is a change or transformation in the traditional contractual clauses, that in essence would have an impact on the country's alignment with the global net zero goals. To achieve strategic alignment in the overall fiscal regime of a country, some of the provisions in oil and gas legislation and

[19] Ibid.

[20] Ibid.

Table 3.2 Types of petroleum agreements

Petroleum agreement	*Description*
Concession (or Licence) Agreements	Concession or licence agreements grant an oil company a right to explore, develop, produce and export the oil extracted in a specified area for which the company has received exclusive development and production rights for a prescribed period. All this is done against the payment of a royalty to the host state. Recent models usually include additional profit taxes and corporate income tax provisions
Production-Sharing Contracts/ Agreements (PSCs/PSAs)	Under the PSA, the host government, as the owner of the resources, engages an international oil company (IOC) as a contractor to provide technical and financial services for exploration and development operations. As a reward for the risks taken, the IOC acquires an entitlement to a stipulated share of the oil produced in the event a commercial discovery is made
Risk Service Agreements	Here, the host state hires the service of a petroleum company or consortium to benefit from its financial and technical expertise. The company or consortium assumes the risk and liability, after which it is reimbursed through a service fee, usually paid in cash
Joint Venture Contracts (JVC)	A JV arises if two or more parties wish to pursue a joint undertaking. It is a partnership-based arrangement between the two parties to jointly run an extractive venture. The agreement provides a structured means for shared decision-making

Source Nalule, V.R., 2021[21]

contracts, which were suitable under business-as-usual (BAU) models will need to be reformed so that they do not hinder energy transition efforts. Although there are several provisions that ought to be discussed, this section will be limited to Environmental provisions; and Legal provisions (stabilisation clauses and arbitration clauses).

[21] Nalule, V.R., *Land Law and the Extractive Industries: Challenges and Opportunities in Africa* (Hart Publishers, 2021).

Environmental Provisions
As earlier discussed, fossil fuels are the main contributor to the GHG emissions. It therefore becomes imperative for the extractive contracts to include environmental provisions aimed at protecting humans, nature and the environment. These could also be reflected in the provisions mandating oil companies to use cleaner and low-carbon resource production technologies such as remote sensing or carbon capture technologies in their operations and adoption of efficiency standards to reduce the emission of GHGs from production activities. Additionally, environmental provisions that align with the net-zero goals could also emphasise the imposition of carbon pricing and/or taxes as a contractual requirement. Below, we review the UK example and analyse the effectiveness of its environmental provisions as contained in the petroleum agreement.

A. United Kingdom[22]:

Section 23: Avoidance of Harmful Methods of Working
23. -(1) The Licensee shall maintain all apparatus and appliances and all Wells in the Licensed Area which have not been abandoned and plugged as provided by clause 19 of this licence in good repair and condition and shall execute all operations in or in connection with the Licensed Area in a proper and workmanlike manner in accordance with methods and practice customarily used in good oilfield practice and without prejudice to the generality of the foregoing provision the Licensee shall take all steps practicable in order-

(a) to control the flow and to prevent the escape or waste of Petroleum discovered in or obtained from the Licensed Area;
(b) to conserve the Licensed Area for productive operations;
(c) to prevent damage to adjoining Petroleum-bearing strata;
(d) (d) to prevent the entrance of water through Wells to Petroleum-bearing strata except for the purposes of secondary recovery; and
(e) to prevent the escape of Petroleum into any waters in or in the vicinity of the Licensed Area.

[22] Shell U.K. Limited, TotalEnergies E&P UK Limited, P2604, Exploitation License, Exploration License, 2021.

B. B. Guyana PSA.[23]

> **Article 28**
> 28.3: The contractor shall take necessary and adequate precautions, in accordance with good international petroleum industry practice, against pollution and for the protection of the environment and the living resources of the river and sea.

The contractual provision relating to environmental protection are visible in different petroleum agreements, as illustrated in the UK and Guyana example above. Whereas these provisions encourage the use of good international petroleum industry practice, to ensure that humans and the environment are not impacted by the adverse impact of petroleum operations, there are no mention of climate-related initiatives aimed at achieving the global net-zero goals. For instance, as earlier mentioned, in addition to the ordinary environmental provisions in petroleum agreements, it would be advisable for the inclusion of provisions relating to mandatory use of clean technologies such as carbon capture and storage (CCS).

Taking an example of the UK, we note that the oil and gas as sector accounts for over three-quarters of the country's total primary energy needs. Between 2014 and 2019, oil and gas production in the UK Continental Shelf increased by 19% and by 2020, almost 46 billion barrels of oil equivalent had been recovered.[24] The oil and gas sector still play a pivotal role in the UK energy mix. In 2021, it accounted for 76% of the country's energy demand.[25] Economically, the sector has contributed to almost £400 billion in oil and gas production taxes since 1970.[26]

[23] See, Petroleum Agreement between the Government of the Cooperative Republic of Guyana and Esso Exploration and Production Guyana Ltd; CNOOC Nexen Petroleum Guyana Ltd and Hess Guyana Exploration Ltd, 2016.

[24] UK EITI, 'Oil & Gas in the UK', https://www.ukeiti.org/oil-gas.

[25] Digest of UK Energy Statistics (DUKES) (2022), table 1.1, Aggregate energy balances, July 2022 (Includes 'primary oils', 'petroleum products' and 'natural gas'), https://www.gov.uk/government/statistics/energy-chapter-1-digest-of-united-kingdomenergy-statistics-dukes.

[26] Offshore Energies UK economic report (2022)—https://oeuk.org.uk/product/economic-report-2022/.

In 2020, the sector accounted for 117,000 direct and indirect jobs in 2020.[27] However, the finite nature of the extractive resources, coupled with their negative impact on the environment, necessitates the need to ensure that the resources are exploited in a manner that aligns with the net-zero goals.

Whereas in recent years, the country has expressed its continued support for the North Sea oil and gas explorations, there have been initiatives to ensure that the activities align with the climate change and net-zero targets. Although not incorporated in the petroleum agreements, specifically the environmental provisions as illustrated in Section 23 above,[28] the UK government initiated the oil and gas checkpoint. This is intended to ensure that ministers are guided by climate related targets before endorsing a prospective licensing round.

A question as to whether the checkpoint is effective in addressing the gaps in the oil and gas contracts, remain to be addressed. This would also depend on the ability of the policy makers to practically enforce the checklist in the petroleum industry. The main aim of the checklist is to ensure that the future licensing rounds are compatible with the UK's climate objectives. The checkpoint is structured with a focus on three tests as illustrated in Table 3.3.

Besides the checklist above, there have been efforts by the North Sea Transition Deal (NSTD) to ensure compliance with the 2015 Paris Agreement and the country's Nationally Determined Contribution (NDC). Carbon budgets have also been introduced to ensure that the country complies with the global net-zero goals. Regarding the petroleum sector, the NSTD data shows that the upstream oil and gas sector is committed to reduce emissions from oil and gas production by 10% by 2025, by 25% by 2027 and by 50% by 2030 (all relative to a 2018 baseline), as measurable steps to a net zero basin by 2050.[29]

The initiatives in the UK as illustrated above, are inspiring. However, regarding the compatibility of the oil and gas contractual provisions with the net-zero goals, there are some gaps to be filled. For instance, it would

[27] Offshore Energies UK, Workforce Insight Report, http://oeuk.org.uk/product/workforce-insight-report-2021, pp. 5, 9.

[28] Shell U.K. Limited, TotalEnergies E&P UK Limited, P2604, Exploitation License, Exploration License, 2021.

[29] North Sea Transition Deal (2021), https://www.gov.uk/government/publications/north-sea-transition-deal.

Table 3.3 Climate compatibility checkpoint design[30]

Reductions in Climate Checkpoint Tests operational greenhouse gas emissions from the sector vs. commitments	This test will compare the performance and projected performance of the UK oil and gas industry against the emissions targets set out by the North Sea Transition Deal (NSTD) which were agreed to by the sector in 2021
Operational greenhouse gas emissions from the sector vs. commitments Operational greenhouse gas emissions intensity from the sector benchmarked internationally	This test benchmarks the UK oil and gas sector against other global producers in terms of associated production emissions
Status of the UK as a net importer of oil and gas	This test evaluates whether the UK is expected to remain a net importer of oil and gas, defined as whether the UK is expected to continue to need to import oil and gas to meet UK energy demand

be advisable for these provisions to provide for mandatory utilisation of clean technologies such as carbon capture and storage.

Additionally, whereas the environmental provisions discourage gas flaring and other activities that negatively impact the environment, it would be prudent for these provision to further specify the emission reduction and efficiency standards to be achieved during petroleum operations in order to advance low carbon transition. Both the contracts signed before 2015 and those signed after 2015, have similar environmental provisions. For instance, the 2003 PSA in Nigeria, while the contract mandates operators to comply with all laws, including the environmental protection law, we note the absence of specific provisions relating to emission reduction and efficiency standards.[31]

[30] Climate Compatibility Checkpoint Design, https://assets.publishing.service.gov.uk/government/uploads/system/uploads/attachment_data/file/1105667/climate-change-checkpoint-design.pdf. Last accessed on 1 September 2023.

[31] See, the Production Sharing Contract between Nigeria National Petroleum Corporation (the Corporation) and Shell Nigeria Ultra Deep Limited (the contractor) covering Block 245 Offshore Nigeria dated 22nd December 2003, doesn't have an Article dedicated to environmental protection.

In Guyana, Article 28 of the PSA provides for environmental protection.[32] It requires the contractor to comply with the Environmental Protection Act, 1996. The article further requires the contractor to take measures to avoid pollution and to ensure the protection of the environment and the living resources of the rivers and sea. In the event of pollution, the contractor is obliged to remedy the impacts. Additionally, in collaboration with the Minister, the contractor is required to establish a program of financial support for environmental and social projects to be funded by the contractor.[33]

From the discussion above, it is clear that the extractive contracts do contain elaborative environmental protection provisions. However, these are not directly related to energy transition or influenced by the net-zero goals. There is no mention of utilising best efforts and environmental protection funds to reduce the project footprint and carbon emissions by incorporating and financing renewable energy projects, both within and surrounding the petroleum projects. Therefore, it is important to have these energy transition expectations expressly provided for in the contracts to ensure compliance. However, besides these provisions, there are also various laws and statutes aimed at protecting the environment as illustrated in the United Kingdom example above.

In addition to the environmental provisions, it is also imperative to assess the effectiveness of the decommissioning laws. Basically, extractive resources are finite, and as such, countries must plan ahead to ensure an efficient, safe, orderly- and environmentally responsible decommissioning of oil and gas facilities. Although most countries are yet to reach the end of their oil and gas life-span, with the global move to transition to a low carbon economy and tackle climate change, it is possible that decommissioning might happen earlier than expected. For example, it is projected that by 2038, more than 1,000 structures and 3,000 wells in the Middle East that were developed in the 1970s will be more than

[32] See, Petroleum Agreement between the Government of the Cooperative Republic of Guyana and Esso Exploration and Production Guyana Ltd; CNOOC Nexen Petroleum Guyana Ltd and Hess Guyana Exploration Ltd, 2016.

[33] Article 28 of the Petroleum Agreement between the Government of the Cooperative Republic of Guyana and Esso Exploration and Production Guyana Ltd; CNOOC Nexen Petroleum Guyana Ltd and Hess Guyana Exploration Ltd, 2016.

30 years old and ready for decommissioning.[34] Decommissioning provisions for onshore are often present in both petroleum contracts and the relevant national petroleum laws, whereas the offshore decommissioning legal framework is determined by international conventions, Regional Conventions, National law and the Host Government Contract. These instruments often have provisions for the establishment of a decommissioning fund.[35] Whereas decommissioning provisions do exist, for relatively new producer countries, the efficiency of these provisions is hard to measure as they have not yet been tested.

Legal Provisions

The main legal provisions in extractive agreements that have an impact on the alignment with net-zero goals include the stabilisation clauses coupled with the arbitration clauses. These provisions will be elaborated on in chapter four of this book.

Stabilisation clauses are contractual assurance of negotiated terms against future legal or regulatory changes.[36] This is achieved by providing legal and fiscal stability.[37] These clauses are mostly found in countries in the Global South as reflected in the Ugandan and Tanzanian example.[38] Other countries such as the Norway and United Kingdom, do not offer stabilisation clauses. Stabilisation clauses target risks that may impact or cause losses to the investors. Such risks include direct expropriation,

[34] Olawuyi, Damilola and Tabbara, Amer, 'Decommissioning in Qatar' in Pereira, Eduardo G. et al. (eds) *The Regulation of Decommissioning, Abandonment and Reuse Initiatives in the Oil and Gas Industry* (Kluwer, 2020), 559–594.

[35] For instance, see Article 6.1 of the Model Timor Leste Onshore Production Sharing Contract, 2014.

[36] Maniruzzaman, A.F.M., 'The Pursuit of Stability in International Energy Investment Contracts: A Critical Appraisal of the Emerging Trends' (2008) 1 *The Journal of World Energy Law & Business*, 121–157, 127. Nr. 2.

[37] Nalule, V.R., 'What Is the Problem with Stabilization Clauses in Petroleum Agreements?' (2022 May 24) 13(1) *Journal of Sustainable Development Law and Policy (The)*, 85–102.

[38] For Tanzania, see, Article 30 (b), of the Model Production Sharing Agreement Between the Government of The United Republic of Tanzania and Tanzania Petroleum Development Corporation and Abc Oil Company, November 2004. For Mozambique see, Articles 27.12, 27.14 of the Exploration and Production Concession Contract between the Government of the Republic of Mozambique and ENI East Africa SpA and Empresa Nacional di Hidrocarbonetos, EP for Area 4 Offshore of the Rovuma Block, Republic of Mozambique 2006.

a gradual loss of investment value by a series of measures over time (creeping expropriation); or the loss of anticipated future opportunities.[39] For the countries that provide for stabilisation clauses, question arises as to whether they have amended them to align with the net-zero goals.

In Mozambique for instance, in their **2018 petroleum agreement,**[40] we note an exclusion in the stabilisation clause. Consequently, while providing for the stability of economic benefits in Article 34.1: Article 34.2 emphasises that the provision on stability does not apply to a change in legislation pertaining to the health, safety, social security or the environment in line with international practice.[41] A similar provision is visible in **Kazakhstan under Article 27, below.**[42]

Article 27: Guarantees of Contract Stability
27.5: The guarantees stipulated in this section shall not be applied to amendments in legislation of the Republic of Kazakhstan related to defence capacity, national security, environmental security and health protection services and taxation.

While the provision above limits contract stability guarantees to among others environmental security, it needs to be rephrased to expressly include energy transition initiatives and climate change responses.

It can be argued that, the earlier version of stabilisation clauses, which coupled with arbitration clauses have led to various energy disputes. In Ghana for instance, the 2004 agreement with Kosmos Energy for the West Cape Three points Block, contains numerous stabilization clauses.

[39] Cameron, P., *International Energy Investment Law: The Pursuit of Stability* (OUP Catalogue, 2010); Olawuyi, Damilola, 'Legal Strategies and Tools for Mitigating Legal Risks Associated with Oil and Gas Investments in Africa' (2015) 39(3) *OPEC Energy Review* (Blackwell Wiley Publishers), 247–265.

[40] Sasol Petroleum Mozambique Exploration Limitada, Empresa Nacional de Hidrocarbonetos, Block PT5-C, PSA, 2018.

[41] Article 34 (2), Sasol Petroleum Mozambique Exploration Limitada, Empresa Nacional de Hidrocarbonetos, Block PT5-C, PSA, 2018.

[42] Contract for Oil and Gas exploration within Zharkamys West-1 blocks XXIII-18 (partially) 19 (partially); XXIV-18 (partially) 19 (partially); XXV-19 (partially) in Aktubinsk Oblast of the Republic of Kazakhstan between the Ministry of Energy and Mineral Resources of the Republic of Kazakhstan and Falcon Oil and Gas Ltd, 2007.

Article 26:2 of the Agreement contains the Guarantee for stability, it states that,

> The State, its departments and agencies, shall support this Agreement and shall take no action which prevents or impedes the due exercise and performance of rights and obligations of the Parties hereunder. As of the Effective Date of this Agreement and throughout its term, the State guarantees Contractor the stability of the terms and conditions of this Agreement as well as the fiscal and contractual framework hereof specifically including those terms and conditions and that framework that are based upon or subject to the provisions of the laws and regulations of Ghana (and any interpretations thereof) including, without limitation, the Petroleum Income Tax Law, the Petroleum Law, the GNPC Law and those other laws, regulations and decrees that are applicable hereto. The State further represent and guarantees that the Contract Area is wholly within Ghana's territorial waters and is not subject to any dispute.

Article 26.4 contains the Balancing/renegotiation clause, it states that,

> Where a Party considers that a significant change in the circumstances prevailing at the time the Agreement was entered into, has occurred affecting the economic balance of the Agreement, the Party adversely affected thereby shall notify the other Parties in writing of the claimed change with a statement of how the claimed change has affected such economic balance or has otherwise affected relations between the Parties. The other Parties shall indicate in writing their reaction to such notification within a period of two (2) months after receipt of such notification. If such significant changes are established by the Parties to have occurred, the Parties shall meet to engage in negotiations and shall effect such changes in, or rectification of, these provisions as they may agree are necessary to restore the relative economic position of the Parties as at the date of this Agreement.

The Ghanian example above, lacks an exclusion clause and as such it is capable of limiting the country's efforts to align its extractive activities with net zero goals. Our analysis shows that some stabilisation clauses especially those negotiated before 2015, do offer wide protection and if there are no exclusion clauses relating to environmental protection, then these can hinder the introduction of energy transitions policies and related initiatives. A case in point is the 2012 Uganda negotiated stabilisation clause stated under Article 33.[43]

From an energy transition perspective, the wider provisions have a likelihood of limiting the host government's powers to introduce special carbon taxes or laws and initiatives relating to carbon pricing in the oil and gas sector. This is because the initiatives would likely impact on the economic value of the project thus resulting in the government paying significant amount of money in damages for breach of contract. Consequently, it is essential for parties to clarify the limitation of such stabilisation clauses. In the contracts, it should be expressly stated that the stabilisation clause does not apply to energy transition policies that might be introduced by the government in a bid to meet its Nationally Determined Contributions (NDCs).

Stabilisation clauses should be read and interpreted in conjunction with arbitration clauses. Most extractive contracts provide for arbitration as a preferred dispute resolution mechanism.[44] However, these provisions are not specifically tailored to address climate and energy transition programs and projects. Additionally, when combined with other clauses such as the Stabilisation clauses, arbitration clauses may limit the host government from introducing energy transition and climate change policies that are in contradiction with other clauses in the petroleum agreement.

The contract provisions in petroleum agreements, therefore, should be amended to provide for expedited national dispute resolution as the first alternative for energy transition and environmental disputes. This will enable Host countries and the related stakeholders address the underlying disputes with the national context fully aligned with the nation's pathway and aspirations.

[43] Production Sharing Agreement for Petroleum Exploration Development and Production in the Republic of Uganda by and between The Government of The Republic of Uganda and Tullow Uganda Limited in respect of the Kanywataba Prospect Area February, 2012. Accessed from UGANDA-KANYWATABA-PSC-FOR-TULLOW.pdf (https://www.africaoilgasreport.com).

[44] See for instance in Ghana, Article 24 of the Model Petroleum Agreement of Ghana (17 August 2000); For Trinidad and Tobago Article 33 of the Deep Onshore Model Production Sharing Contract, 2006; for Uganda, Article 26 of the Production Sharing Agreement for Petroleum Exploration Development and Production in The Republic of Uganda by and between The Government of The Republic of Uganda and Tullow Uganda Limited in respect of Exploration Area 1, February 2012.

3.4 Conclusion

This chapter, referring to different case studies, aimed at surveying the various extractive contracts to ascertain whether they align with the net-zero goals. The extractive contracts and the provisions therein, have prima facie not transformed to address climate change or even align with the net-zero goals. The provisions that existed before the signing of the 2015 Paris Agreement, are similar to those in the current contracts signed after 2015. However, these provisions have to be read and interpreted taking into account the relevant laws and statutes. As illustrated in the UK example, although the environmental provisions do not necessarily specify how the parties to the petroleum agreement are aligning their activities with the country's climate change targets and net-zero goals, there are initiatives such as the climate compatibility checkpoint, that the country is taking and introducing to ensure that oil and gas operations are not an impediment to energy transition.

Besides the environmental and legal provisions, other extractive provisions should also be taken into consideration. For instance, a question may arise as to whether the local content provisions in the extractive contracts are compatible with the net-zero goals? Most countries have introduced local content provisions in their petroleum contracts.[45] Other countries like Nigeria and Angola, have gone ahead to enact local content laws focused on increasing the workforce in the oil and gas sector. These provisions by nature broadly reference the creation of local employment and trainings in the extractive sector, however, they provide no room for the relevant stakeholders to adapt to the ever-changing energy sector, which is now moving towards a low carbon economy. It would be understandable for local content and training provisions to be limited to oil and gas; however, it would also be prudent for such provisions to be revised to ensure that the operators are tasked with taking part in initiatives aimed at creating green jobs, or training on net-zero transition. In this climate change and energy transition era, local content provisions and policies could be leveraged and tailored to emphasise the need for Extractive Companies to establish and implement investment, training and local

[45] For instance, for Trinidad and Tobago, see Article 39 of the Deep Onshore Model Production Sharing Contract, 2006. For Guyana, see, Article 19 of the Petroleum Agreement between the Government of the Cooperative Republic of Guyana and Esso Exploration and Production Guyana Ltd; CNOOC Nexen Petroleum Guyana Ltd and Hess Guyana Exploration Ltd, 2016.

initiatives that increase climate awareness and strengthen the transition to efficient technologies and practices across the entire petroleum sector value chain.

Besides local content provisions, stakeholders could also consider amending the provisions relating to the management committee in petroleum contracts. Most of these provisions have no requirement for inclusion of environmental experts or renewable energy experts.[46] This is so because most of the committees are focused on experts in oil and gas sector. However, it would be prudent to include climate change experts, who can adequately advise on how best the operator can align their activities with the country's net-zero goals. In the next chapter, we analyse the negotiation tools and strategies to address the net-zero risks in extractive contracts.

[46] For instance, In Iraq, see Article 8 of the Production Sharing Contract Topkhana Block Kurdistan Region Between the Kurdistan Regional Government of Iraq and Talisman (Block K39) B.V, 2013.

CHAPTER 4

Negotiation Tools and Strategies to Address Transition Risks in Extractive Contracts

Abstract This chapter examines the negotiation tools and strategies to address transition risks in extractive contracts. As more countries and corporations adopt net zero plans, transition risks—resulting from the introduction of new or more stringent environment, social and governance standards and requirements—are also on the rise. On the one hand, contractual clauses and provisions, such as stabilization and dispute resolution clauses in preexisting long term resource contracts may constrain or states' sovereign rights and abilities to advance net zero. On the other hand, the increasing demand for transition minerals, such as lithium, nickel, uranium, copper amongst others, has fueled a new wave of resource nationalism and unilateral cancellation of mining contracts in many resource-rich countries. There is a clear need for states and investors to reassess and adapt their existing resource contracts to address these and other emerging transition risks in order to avoid legal liability and disputes. This chapter discusses the role of net zero-aligned extractive contracts in addressing transition risks. It examines key contractual clauses

This chapter is co-authored with Umair Dogar, Research Fellow, UNESCO Chair on Environmental Law and Sustainable Development, Hamad bin Khalifa University, Doha, Qatar.

V. R. Nalule et al., *Renegotiating Contracts for the Energy Transition in the Extractives Industry*, Just Transitions,
https://doi.org/10.1007/978-3-031-46258-0_4

that should be negotiated and integrated into extractive contracts to mitigate transition risks. The legal and institutional barriers to renegotiating long term extractive contracts, especially capacity gaps, are also examined, to identify the ways in which extant and new generation of extractive contracts can be better aligned with net zero objectives.

Keywords Extractive contracts · Net zero goals · Contractual adjustments · Institutional quality · Licensing and stabilization clauses

4.1 Introduction

This chapter examines the negotiation tools and strategies to address transition risks in extractive contracts. It discusses the role of net zero-aligned extractive contracts in addressing transition risks. The legal and institutional barriers to renegotiating long term extractive contracts, especially capacity gaps, are also examined, in order to identify the ways in which extant and new generation of extractive contracts can be better aligned with net zero objectives.

Growing environmental, social and governance (ESG) requirements—either through long term governmental policies, regulations or standardized industry guidelines—have significantly increased the focus on the energy transition, driving demand away from fossil fuels and towards transition minerals required for net zero economies.[1] The ambitions and pledges to transition toward net zero are already resulting in increased divestments from coal, oil and gas projects, while resulting in increased investment in renewable and decarbonization projects, especially solar, wind, hydro and storage technologies and infrastructure projects.[2] At the same time, several countries are also emphasizing more stringent resource efficiency and climate-smart infrastructure standards, such as net zero

[1] Olawuyi D., and Athwal, E., 'ESG Considerations for Midstream and Downstream Oil and Gas' in Pereira, Eduardo, Talus Kim, and de Gyarfas, Vera (eds) *Encyclopaedia of Midstream and Downstream Oil and Gas* (Globe Law and Business Ltd, 2022).

[2] Share Action, 'HSBC Announces It Will No Longer Finance New Oil and Gas Fields—Share Action Response' (2022), https://shareaction.org/news/hsbc-announces-it-will-no-longer-finance-new-oil-and-gas-fields-shareaction-response?token=IcQ5WS9tht8-TEEQvxuwEDe-2weKKnYd&s=09, accessed 1 May 2023.

buildings.[3] For instance, climate-related financial disclosures (TCFD) are increasingly becoming commonplace which require companies to report on the direct and indirect effects of climate change.[4] This is effectively raising the momentum for increased calls and demand for states and investors to ensure a just transition, in a manner that leaves no group, persons or communities behind.[5] Studies already show how stabilization provisions in extractive contracts, which freeze the abilities of states to update existing laws or contracts, may constrain regulatory space for governments to advance net zero or to achieve a just transition.[6] As of December 2022, more than 2000 climate and net zero related cases have been filed in 65 jurisdictions and international or regional courts and tribunals, with some cases specifically challenging net zero and energy transition targets as breach of contract or investment expropriation.[7] Cases challenging extractive companies for greenwashing and misleading

[3] Addison, T., 'Climate Change and the Extractives Sector' in *Extractive Industries: The Management of Resources as a Driver of Sustainable Development* (Oxford University Press, 2018); Zillman, D., Roggenkamp, M., Paddock, L., and Godden, L. 'Introduction: How Technological and Legal Innovation Are Transforming Energy Law' in Zillman, D., Roggenkamp, M., Paddock, L., and Godden, L. (eds) *Innovation in Energy Law and Technology: Dynamic Solutions for Energy Transitions* (Oxford University Press, 2018), 1–16.

[4] Vizcarra, H.V., 'Climate-Related Disclosure and Litigation Risk in the Oil & Gas Industry: Will State Attorneys General Investigations Impede the Drive for More Expansive Disclosures? (2019) 43 *Vermont Law Review*, 733–735.

[5] Addison (n. 219), Olawuyi, D., 'Climate Justice and Corporate Responsibility: Taking Human Rights Seriously in Climate Actions and Projects' (2016) 34(1) *Journal of Energy & Natural Resources Law*, 27–44.

[6] Natural Resource Governance Institute, 'Tying Their Hands? How Petroleum Contract Terms May Limit Governments' Climate Policy Flexibility' (2021), https://resourcegovernance.org/analysis-tools/publications/tying-their-hands-how-petroleum-contract-terms-may-limit-gov-climate-policy-flexibility, accessed 27 August 2023.

[7] United Nations Environment Programme, 'Global Climate Litigation Report: 2023 Status Review' (2023), https://climate.law.columbia.edu/content/global-climate-litigation-report-2023-statusreview#:~:text=This%20Global%20Climate%20Litigation%20Report,global%20climate%20change%20litigation%20trends. See also Westmoreland Mining Holdings v Canada, ICSID Case No UNCT/20/3; *RWE AG and RWE Eemshaven Holding II BV v. Kingdom of the Netherlands (ICSID Case No. ARB/21/4)* seeking €1.4 billion in compensation for "expropriation of their investments."

net zero disclosures are also fast rising.[8] There are reputational and financial costs arising from litigation, regulatory non-compliance, and adverse publicity with the increasing pressure on extractives companies to incorporate ESG requirements into their strategic plans, environmental and social impact assessments, safety management systems, and engineering practices.[9] The widening nature and scope of ESG requirements call for a reimagination of natural resource contracts both to ensure compliance with the evolving ESG standards, as well as to advance net zero and energy transition in extractive activities and projects.[10]

For the extractive sector to advance net zero and the energy transition, net zero-aligned extractive contracts are required. Net zero-aligned extractive contracts are contracts that not only address the wide range of legal and contractual risks and liabilities that are emerging from the ongoing energy transition, but also remove barriers to accelerating a just, inclusive, and orderly energy transition that leaves no one behind. This chapter examines the guiding principles of aligning extractive contracts with net zero objectives. After this introduction, Sect. 4.2 delves into the specific elements of net zero-aligned extractive contracts in a rapidly changing extractive industry in the face of rising ESG requirements. Section 4.4 highlights the legal and institutional barriers in resource-abundant countries to adequately address the challenge of aligning extractive contracts specifically and the extractive industry generally to net zero. Section 4.5 proposes legal strategies and tools for addressing the barriers. Section 4.6 is the concluding section.

[8] See Clean Energy Wire, 'Environmental NGO Wins Greenwashing Lawsuit Against TotalEnergies' (2023), https://www.cleanenergywire.org/news/environmental-ngo-wins-greenwashing-lawsuit-against-totalenergies; also *Advertising Standards Authority UK v Shell UK Ltd*, ASA Ruling on Shell UK Ltd.'s Shell Go+ Campaign, Advertising Standards Authority, 8 July 2020 (United Kingdom of Great Britain and Northern Ireland), https://www.asa.org.uk/rulings/shell-uk-ltd-g22-1170842-shell-uk-ltd.html, accessed 28 August 2023.

[9] Addison (n. 219), 470–471.

[10] Talus, Kim, 'Adapting International Natural Gas and LNG Agreements in the Light of the Energy Transition' (2023) *Journal of World Energy Law and Business*, 1–16.

4.2 Nature, Scope and Elements of Net Zero-Aligned Extractive Contracts

Extractive contracts have for many decades provided a bedrock for states to allocate rights and interests in the development of their extractive resources.[11] Ranging from production sharing contract (PSC), joint venture contract (JVC), joint operating agreements, service agreements, to participation agreements such a farmout contracts, pooling and unitization contracts, sale and purchase agreements, transportation contracts, and community or impact benefit agreements, these contracts are pivotal to the extractive industry.[12] Irrespective of the regulatory regime in place or the type of contract used, the investor always aims to maximize the profitability and sustainability of the investment while minimizing regulatory risks. On the other hand, the host state aims to maximize revenue from its natural resources by ensuring it remains attractive to foreign investors and avoiding adverse social, human rights, and environmental side effects in the process. The rise of transition risks in the extractive sector for the state and the investor alike has added an additional dimension to the balancing act between the objectives of resource-rich states and investors.

Since the adoption of the Paris Agreement in 2015, there has been a growing consensus among legal scholars that the nature long term contracts in the extractive sector, and the associated disputes and challenges flowing from them, may constrain the pace of the clean energy transition.[13] Several of the extractive sector contracts were adopted many years before the Paris Agreement, and before countries began to elaborate net zero plans. Without aligning long term extractive contracts with the net zero pledges and plans adopted by resource rich countries, it would be difficult to achieve coherence in net zero efforts, and to avoid legal disputes and risk that may result from net zero programs and policies.

[11] Olawuyi, D.S., *Extractives Industry Law in Africa* (Cham: Springer International Publishing, 2018), 191–195.

[12] Ibid., also Kienzler D. et al., 'Natural Resource Contracts as a Tool for Managing the Mining Sector' (2015) 43.

[13] Talus (n. 226). See also Natural Resource Governance Institute (n. 222); Boute (2021) 339; Brauch, M.D., & Toledano, P., 'Integrating Climate Change, Decarbonization, and Just Transition Considerations into Extractive Industry Contracts' (June 15, 2022), https://ccsi.columbia.edu/news/climate-change-decarbonization-just-transition-mining-oil-gas-contracts.

4.3 Key Contractual Clauses of Extractive Contracts to Address Transition Risks

There is a plethora of literature on the transition risks faced by the extractive industry, state and investor alike.[14] Nevertheless, the adoption of net zero-aligned clauses in state-investor contracts remain slow. In jurisdictions where contractual agreements are the primary fiscal tool in regulating the extractive industry, as stated above, it is imperative that extractive contracts include specific clauses to promote sustainable, climate-friendly extractive practices, especially regulating the transition-related impacts and contributions of extractive projects.[15]

4.3.1 *Prospect of Renegotiation in Long-Term Extractive Contracts*

The lifecycle of an extractive industry project can span up to twenty or thirty years. Consequently, projects are traditionally long-term owing to the timescale associated with each phase of such a project from reconnaissance, discovery to extraction.[16] Consequently, extractive contracts are traditionally long-term as well. The inherent limitation in the face of rising transition risks is the lock-in effect created through long-term extractive contracts whereby the buyer is unable to transition to a more sustainable source of energy despite a governmental ban on natural gas production or exports or the buyer's own preference.[17] The potential recourse is either mutual termination or one party's willingness to pay for the cancelation of the contract. Alternatively, if the contract also contains a periodic review

[14] Among many others, Olawuyi, D., 'Can MENA Extractive Industries Support the Global Energy Transition? Current Opportunities and Future Directions' (2020) *Extractives Industry and Society Journal*, https://doi.org/10.1016/j.exis.2020.02.003, Oyewunmi, T., Crossley, P., Sourgens F., and Talus K. (eds), *Decarbonisation and the Energy Industry: Law, Policy and Regulation in Low-Carbon Energy Markets* (Hart Publishing, 2020); also Brauch and Toledano, ibid.

[15] Mebratu-Tsegaye, Tehtena, Toledano, Perrine, Brauch, Martin Dietrich, and Greenberg, Mara, *Five Years After the Adoption of the Paris Agreement, Are Climate Change Considerations Reflected in Mining Contracts?* (Columbia Center on Sustainable Investment [CCSI], 2021), 6, https://ccsi.columbia.edu/sites/default/files/content/docs/ccsi-climate-change-investor-state-mining-contracts.pdf.

[16] Olawuyi (n. 227).

[17] Talus (n. 226).

clause, it may provide the parties a certain degree of flexibility to renegotiate key terms of the contract to ensure that contractual performance that is otherwise threatened by transition risks can be remedied.[18]

From the investor's perspective, negotiation is an uncertain, expensive, and time-consuming process especially if the state lacks institutional capacity. Especially since negotiations can result in flawed agreements because the state lacked the capacity to undertake effective feasibility studies or asset valuations. Investors may therefore be wary of renegotiating a contract irrespective of the circumstances since it could result in project and investment uncertainty. However, the sanctity of existing long-term contracts should not preclude the ability to make necessary corrections in light of latest knowledge and emerging industry best practices.[19] This can be achieved through the inclusion of time-based or event-triggered periodic review clauses to acknowledge and account for the fact that changes can occur in a long-term project and thus it is necessary to create a mechanism that allows renegotiating the contract in good faith and in light of impending transition risks so that parties can collectively hedge against potential losses that may be incurred. A periodic review clause also acknowledges that a natural resource project is a long and collaborative process and that a strong working relationship takes precedence over short-term wins during negotiations.[20]

4.3.2 Arbitration Clause

The rise of transition risks has, naturally, resulted in a rising number of wide-ranging disputes. As the extractive industry landscape changes due to ESG regulations and standards to protect and further the public interest, so do the economic viability of projects from the investor's perspective. Therefore, the importance of a clear and enforceable arbitration clause cannot be overemphasized. On the flipside, scholars have posited, based on the widespread use of arbitration clauses in investor-state extractive contracts, arbitration can have unintended and undesirable consequences like undermining state sovereignty, regulatory space and

[18] Kienzler et al. (n. 228) 43.

[19] Ibid.

[20] Ibid.

the rule of law.[21] Arbitrator discretion over interpretation and application of the law of the host state has resulted in overriding the public interest-focused determinations of regulatory and administrative agencies.[22]

It is imperative that the new forms of disputes relating to transition risks are dealt with through clear and comprehensive arbitration clauses that allow for the fair, timely and effective to avoid costly delays to time-sensitive transition projects.[23] There is a need to avoid uncertainties and ambiguities that may result in procedural challenges and delay arbitration. In addition to specificity relating to the rules, language, seat and venue of arbitration, energy transition projects often involve multiple contracts and parties, so there is a need to provide for the consolidation and joining of multiple arbitration in case of disputes through an umbrella dispute resolution contract.[24] Furthermore, given the complex and evolving nature of the energy transition, there is also a need to provide for expert determination of technical issues relating to climate change and the energy transition. For example, expert opinion may be required to properly quantify, verify and assess climate related obligations, such as GHG emission compliance, emission credits, communicating climate related programs to avoid greenwashing and misleading statements amongst others.

4.3.3 *Just Transition Clause*

Debates on just transition aim to ensure that the implementation of net zero and clean energy transition projects proceed in a manner that respects and promotes human rights, with meaningful participation of all people regardless of income, race, colour, creed, or national origin or

[21] Johnson, Lise, Guven, Brooke, and Coleman, Jesse, "Investor-State Dispute Settlement: What Are We Trying to Achieve? Does ISDS Get Us There?" *Columbia Center on Sustainable Investment* (CCSI) (blog), December 11, 2017, https://ccsi.columbia.edu/news/investor-state-dispute-settlement-what-are-we-trying-achieve-does-isds-get-us-there.

[22] Ibid.

[23] Talus (n. 222).

[24] See Delaney, Joachim et al., 'Disputes Arising Out of Energy Transition Projects in Australia' (2022), https://globalarbitrationreview.com/review/the-asia-pacific-arbitration-review/2023/article/disputes-arising-out-of-energy-transition-projects-in-australia.

other status.[25] Just transition draws on longstanding principles relating to climate justice, energy justice and environmental justice all of which require that energy transition programs should not result in disproportionate burdens, social exclusions, poverty, marginalization or other adverse human rights impacts for any community, group or peoples, especially at-risk groups such as women, youth, Indigenous peoples, and workers in emissions-intensive sectors. The just energy transition debate is particularly crucial for the extractive sector, in light of growing reports that net zero programs are already resulting in significant job loss and reduced employment for workers in the extractive sector.[26] The Paris Agreement therefore expressly recognises the 'imperatives of a just transition of the workforce,' and the need for all Parties to 'respect, promote and consider their respective obligations on human rights' when taking action to address climate change.[27]

While just transition clauses are gaining increased use in construction and manufacturing sectors,[28] such clauses are yet to gain widespread recognition and adoption in extractive contracts, including those negotiated after the adoption of the Paris Agreement in 2015. To advance a just and inclusive energy transition, there is a need for modern extractive contracts to include a just transition clause. A just transition clause will identify the obligation of investors and state to comprehensively evaluate, through mandatory human rights due diligence, the likely impact of net zero programs and efforts of at-risks groups, and to demonstrate targeted programs to address such adverse impacts. This will include the need for extractive sector investors to proactively monitor and disclose measures aimed at advancing gender justice, environmental justice and

[25] See United Nations Working Group on Business and Human Rights (2023), 'Extractive Sector, Just Transition and Human Rights' (2023) UN General Assembly Report, also Heffron, R., 'The Role of Justice in Developing Critical Minerals' (2020) 7 *The Extractive Industries and Society*, 855.

[26] Saget, Catherine et al., *Jobs in a Net-Zero Emissions Future in Latin America and the Caribbean* (Inter-American Development Bank and International Labour Organization, 2020).

[27] See Preamble to the Paris Agreement, also Articles 2.2 and 4.1.

[28] The Chancery Lane Project, 'Just Transition in Climate Clauses' (last updated 3 November 2022), https://chancerylaneproject.org/wp-content/uploads/2022/11/Just-Transition-in-Climate-Clauses-V1.pdf, accessed 10 June 2023.

energy justice in the design, approval and implementation of clean energy transition programs.[29]

4.3.4 Stabilization Clause

There is immense literature on the stabilization clause as it is increasingly relied upon by investors to invoke breach of contract when regulators introduce measures to incentivize more sustainable sources of energy instead of extractive operations.[30] Stabilization clauses either freeze the regulatory landscape at the time the contract is entered into—as an assurance to the investor that the investment is shielded from any unpredictable legal, regulatory or political change that may affect the commercial viability of the project—or compensate the investor for the financial impacts of any new or modified legislation.[31] The direct impact of an overbearing stabilization clause is the inability of the state to enact new legislation and in the current climate of transition risks, it hinders states from introducing any regulatory measures in a rapidly changing world. There is increasing literature discouraging the use altogether of such clauses due to the marked disadvantage they pose to the regulator. The long-standing belief on use of stabilization clauses was that it helped attract foreign investment as it was considered necessary by investors to seek guarantees for the profitability of long-term projects in the face of changes in the regulatory landscape.[32]

Studies have cited the lack of flexibility that stabilization clauses afford governments in responding to environmental, economic or political development goals generally and transition risks specifically and discouraged their use.[33] Furthermore, restrictive stabilization clauses may also

[29] See United Nations Working Group on Business and Human Rights (n. 241).

[30] See Nalule, V., 'What Is the Problem with Stabilization Clauses in Petroleum Agreements?' (2022) 13(1) *Journal of Sustainable Development Law and Policy*, 85–102.

[31] Natural Resource Governance Institute (n. 222); Kienzler et al. (n. 228) 47.

[32] Ibid.

[33] The Organization for Economic Cooperation and Development (OECD), United Nations, and the International Monetary Fund, among others, have issued policy positions stating that stabilization clauses may cause more harm by limiting the ability of states to implement necessary regulatory changes while achieving little in attracting foreign investment. See specifically, of the OECD (2020), principle VII; also see United Nations Working Group on Business and Human Rights (n. 241).

restrict the abilities of states to attract new technologies and investments, including ESTs needed to advance the energy transition.[34] In the event that a state has to implement necessary policy changes, an overbearing stabilization clause will undermine the contract. Therefore, it is in the best interest of parties to either avoid the stabilization clause altogether or limit its application to fiscal provisions i.e. taxes, royalties, and the like, and its duration not so long that the investor is exempt from any changes in regulations for two to three decades. Instead, stabilization clauses should be long enough to provide the investor assurance to recover the cost of the investment along with a reasonable return.[35] Alternatively, parties can agree to a mandatory negotiation if a change in law results in the investor facing difficulty in meeting its contractual obligations i.e. an event that trigger the periodic review clause.

4.3.5 *Force Majeure Clause*

The force majeure clause is another boilerplate provision that only recently started receiving much attention due to the COVID-19 pandemic. This clause excuses a party from contractual performance as a result of reasonably unforeseeable circumstances beyond the party's control and prevent or hinder it from performing its contractual obligations.[36] Traditionally, a force majeure clause has included a list of events that provide parties the grounds to invoke this clause and excuse themselves from contractual performance. These include extreme weather events while sometimes specifying that these are reasonably unforeseeable. The increasing frequency of extreme weather events along with the increasing accuracy and robustness of climate data, it is difficult to invoke the force majeure clause due to a reasonably unforeseeable extreme weather event. From the perspective of the state to address transition risks in its extractive contracts, the force majeure clause should no longer include climate-related events and focus on the foreseeability and reasonableness of preventing physical impacts of such events on extractive operations and surrounding communities instead of the foreseeability

[34] Ibid. Also NRGI (n. 222).

[35] Kienzler et al. (n. 228) 47.

[36] Boute, A., 'Environmental Force Majeure: Relief from Fossil Energy Contracts in the Decarbonisation Era' (2021) 33(2) *Journal of Environmental Law*, 339.

to prevent the extreme weather event from occurring.[37] Additionally, the contract should require investors to conduct thorough climate risk assessments and embed climate resilience in project design, construction and operations as climate change events can no longer be characterized as unforeseeable.[38]

4.4 Legal and Institutional Barriers to Negotiating Net Zero-Aligned Extractive Contracts

Despite the growing realization of the need for net-zero aligned extractive contracts that ensure coherence of extractive contracts with growing net zero ambitions, progress remains slows in many countries. This section discusses some of the key hindrances to the reimagination of extractive contracts to make them net-zero aligned. Understanding the challenges can help states, and investors alike, to develop innovative and risk-informed approaches that can enhance effective risk mitigation and management.

4.4.1 Constraining Clauses in Existing Contracts

The nexus of stabilization, force majeure, and dispute resolution clauses play a decisive role in hindering the ability of states to enact and adopt laws and regulations that will help with the transition to a net zero economy and effectively address climate-related risks to their extractives industry. Specifically, as discussed earlier in this chapter, contractual clauses, if not net-zero aligned properly, can act as legal barriers by constraining the host state from introducing legislation that would help align its extractives industry to address transition risks adequately. State sovereignty in this regard is often further undermined through investment treaties. There is therefore an urgent need for resource rich countries

[37] Brauch, M.D., Toledano, Perrine, and Aceveda, Cody, *Allocation of Climate-Related Risks in Investor–State Mining Contracts* (New York: Columbia Center on Sustainable Investment (CCSI), June 2022), https://ccsi.columbia.edu/content/allocation-climate-change-risks-investor-state-mining-contracts, 5–6, also Natural Resource Governance Institute (n. 222), 4–7.

[38] Natural Resource Governance Institute (n. 222), 4–7.

to reevaluate and renegotiate their existing long-term contracts to bring them in alignment with net zero targets and ambitions.

Furthermore, despite the increased recognition of just transition concerns in the extractive sector, just transition clauses are yet to gain widespread recognition and adoption in extractive contracts. As earlier discussed, there is a need to integrate just transition clauses in extractive contracts so as to specifically highlight the obligation of investors and state-owned enterprise to address the wide range of human rights impacts associated with the energy transition and to promote just and inclusive transition programs that leaves no one behind.

4.4.2 *No Climate Change or Net Zero Laws in Many Countries Resulting in Contractual Gaps*

As stated earlier in this chapter, the ideal tool to address transition risks faced by the extractive industry is a robust regulatory framework on climate change and net zero. Such legislative clarity can enable extractive sector investors to better understand ESG obligations, especially those relating to GHG emission reduction, just transition, climate disclosure and capacity development. For example, Nigeria's Climate Change Act of 2021 mandates every private business or entity with more than 50 employees to submit annual carbon emission reduction targets, and to appoint Climate Change Officer or an Environmental Sustainability Officer. Failure to comply will result in a fine.[39] Such legislative clarity can enable extractive investors to properly quantify and price ESG compliance costs at contract negotiation stages.

However, only few countries have enacted clear and comprehensive climate change laws, while majority of the resource-abundant countries face the challenge to design and implement necessary net zero regulations and laws.[40] A robust regulatory framework is stringent, promotes transparency and reduces regulatory failure and improves the degree of compliance, while also assigning responsibilities for implementation across

[39] See Article 24 of the Nigerian Climate Change Act, 2021.

[40] Addison (2018). For example, Kenya also enacted the Climate Change Act on May 2016. For other efforts across the Global South, see *The Climate Change Laws of the World Database*, https://climate-laws.org, accessed 27 August 2023 (hereafter *Climate Change Laws Database*).

ministries and administrative agencies.[41] The first step to developing domestic laws on climate change and net zero economies is the development of a vision and policy on energy transition. Typically, when a new mineral or energy resource is discovered by a state with limited exposure to the regulation of the extractives sector, politics favor short-term gains over building regulatory systems that protect the public interest in the long run.[42] Natural resource discoveries are inherently associated with uncertainties and lengthy delays and production rarely starts immediately. Whereas, high quality strategic decision making that can be translated into a robust regulatory framework to support investments, further public interest and address transition risks requires a skillful and independent civil service and consensus among political elites.[43]

4.4.3 Lack of Institutional Capacity

In order to develop a robust regulatory framework that supports net zero-aligned extractive contracts, domestic capacity in the extractive sector from a climate change and transition risk perspective is imperative. The quality of personnel is imperative to the quality of the institutions that employ them and the regulations to implement. Resource-abundant states, especially in developing countries, often lack specialist personnel and technical resources needed to design, implement and manage a comprehensive regulatory system in a highly specialized extractive industry with many technical dimensions.[44] In specific terms, the skills available to the regulatory bodies need to match those available to the investors in the project life cycle of the extractive industry starting from negotiations to implementation of closure plans. Although host states have the option to hire industry experts to assist with negotiation of contracts and development of regulatory frameworks, it is still

[41] Babalola, A., and Olawuyi, D., 'Overcoming Regulatory Failure in the Design and Implementation of Gas Flaring Policies: The Potential and Promise of an Energy Justice Approach' (2022) 14(11) *Sustainability*.

[42] Ibid.

[43] Ibid.

[44] Ibid. See also Aubynn, T., 'Regulatory Structures and Challenges to Developmental Extractives: Some Practical Observations from Ghana' in Addison et al. (eds) *Extractive Industries: The Management of Resources as a Driver of Sustainable Development* (Oxford University Press, 2018).

necessary for host states to have significant in-house expertise to spot, evaluate and address transition risks in a timely and effective manner and to protect public interest. Without bridging capacity gaps, resource rich countries may continue to negotiate lopsided extractive contracts that do not advance net zero objectives, or that constrain their abilities to avoid a new surge of resource curse that could be associated with the ongoing rush for transition minerals.[45]

4.5 Toward Net Zero Aligned Extractive Contracts: Recommendations

While there is a growing recognition on the need to renegotiate and adapt extractive contracts with net zero targets, the practical aspects of achieving such net-zero aligned extractive contracts remains complex in many countries. Lack of political will to advance the net zero transition, as well as capacity gaps in contract negotiation to integrate transparency and right-based requirements relating to just transition, remain widespread.

There is an urgent need for regulators, investors and industry associations to collaborate and develop model contracts that effectively address transition risks in the extractives industry. Such model contracts would integrate clauses that ensure and enable an energy transition that is timely, just, sustainable, and efficient. In the absence of robust regulatory frameworks, these model contracts should provide stop-gap measures through provisions centered on adaptation measures requiring climate risk, community vulnerability, and human rights impact assessments for all extractive industry projects and investments. This will be in addition to integration of climate risks and just transition aspects into closure or decommissioning plans by requiring companies to earmark resources at the outset of a project for all associated socioeconomic and environmental risks and impacts of the extractive project.[46] From a mitigation perspective, the model contract should require investors to use renewable energy sources, estimate and disclose GHG emissions, and adopt governance structures that incentivize climate action. On a general level, extractive contracts should not contain any clauses that constrain the host state's

[45] Nyer, D., and Marchili, S. 'A New Wave of Resource Nationalism in the Mining & Metals Industry' (2021), https://www.whitecase.com/insight-our-thinking/new-wave-resource-nationalism-mining-metals-industry, accessed 27 August 2023.

[46] Brauch and Toledano (n. 229); See Forabosco, Andrea and others (2022).

ability in adopting laws and regulations to reduce transition risks from extractive projects. Model contracts should require investors to purchase those insurance policies that use effective tools to accurately measure transition risks i.e., parametric insurance that can make a pre-determined payment within days or even in advance of the adverse event taking place.[47] Finally, contractual provisions should also be used to enable innovative technological solutions to enable immediate and seamless physical risk transfer.

Collaboration between investors, regulators and other stakeholders across the extractive industry can also play a pivotal role in addressing the lack of institutional capacity among resource-abundant states. This can be achieved through knowledge sharing on the principles of net zero economies, internationally recognized industry standards and best practices. Additionally, targeted capacity-building programs should be developed focused on contract negotiation and implementation, and policy development and management. The recipients of these capacity-building programs should not only include the civil service but also members of the judiciary, bar associations, and domestic industry associations. The success of these capacity-building programs should be measured on their ability to equip the local populace with sufficient skillset to enact its own robust legal framework that capably protects the public interest while addressing transition risks in a rapidly changing extractive industry.

4.6 Conclusion

As countries and business enterprises worldwide release net zero and energy transition plans and programs, extractive sector contracts will play key roles both in ensuring the supply of energy transition minerals needed for such transition, as well as in advancing a just, inclusive, and orderly transition that leaves no one behind. As new forms of ESG risks continue to challenge the abilities of extractive sector investors to maintain risk free investments in the sector, there is a need to address contractual obstacles to a just transition through careful renegotiation to achieve net-zero aligned contractual frameworks. Extractive sector investors must also re-evaluate and mitigate their exposure to increasing resource nationalism, stringent ESG requirements, as well as new net zero

[47] Brauch and Toledano (n.229); The Chancery Lane Project (2023).

infrastructure requirements that may increase investment and compliance costs. Negotiating net zero aligned extractive contracts will go a long way to comprehensively address clauses that hinder transparent and effective risk management with respect to net zero, just transition and mandatory human rights due diligence in the extractive sector.

The task of renegotiating and implementing net zero and climate-aligned natural resource contracts must start with addressing barriers in existing laws and contracts that may hinder such alignment process. First is the need for a national strategy and policy that aligns investment frameworks with net zero ambitions. This will set the stage for harmonizing the wide range of legislation and standards in the extractive sector in a manner that achieves coherence and consistency. This harmonization will cut across fiscal frameworks and regulations, as well as transparency and disclosure regulations. For example, extractive industry transparency initiatives will need to provide guidelines on measuring, disclosing, and reporting net zero programs in the extractive sector in a transparent manner that eliminates greenwashing. Such guidelines will not only place an obligation on extractive sector investors to advance net zero, but to also publish and disclose just transition related investments, opportunities, and risks across their entire value chain. Furthermore, to avoid resource curse associated with surging demand for transition minerals, there is a need to infuse extractive contracts with transparency requirements, to ensure that transition minerals are sourced legitimately and in a manner that respects human rights and minimizes conflicts and modern slavery.

There is also a need for industry-wide collaboration to promote capacity and knowledge acquisition on negotiating net zero aligned extractive contracts. In addition to promoting model clauses and contracts relating to just transition, stabilization, dispute resolution, and force majeure provisions amongst others, there is a need for industry associations to develop targeted training programs in this regard. Bridging extant capacity gaps on net zero aligned contracts, especially in developing countries, will require international cooperation and solidarity aimed at enhancing targeted education, knowledge development, acquisition and awareness on negotiating and integrating net zero obligations in resource contracts. Higher education institutions, especially law faculties also have key roles to play in introducing tailored courses on net zero aligned energy contracts which will introduce the fundamentals of allocating and managing transition related ESG risks in a net zero era.

CHAPTER 5

Conclusion and Future Directions

Abstract As countries are battling with climate change impacts, they are also concerned with energy poverty impacts including an escalation in deforestation, which is triggered by the continued reliance on traditional energy such as biomass. It has proved hard to have a wholesome energy transition, necessitating scholars to recognise the progressive nature of energy use, which has been termed Energy Progression. Countries in both the global north and global south are therefore faced with the twin challenge of addressing energy security and climate change while also ensuring that there is a just transition to a low-carbon economy. This chapter therefore, gives policy direction on how to address the energy transition risks; how to renegotiate extractive contracts for the energy transition.

Keywords Energy transition · Climate change · Energy access · Energy progression · Energy justice · Extractives · Net zero

This book has brought to light the dilemma of addressing the inherent risks with climate change and ensuring energy security. These two issues are indeed given attention in the UN SDGs 13 and 7 respectively. As illustrated in the introductory chapter, climate change impacts have been experienced in different countries all across the world recently. This has

V. R. Nalule et al., *Renegotiating Contracts for the Energy Transition in the Extractives Industry*, Just Transitions,
https://doi.org/10.1007/978-3-031-46258-0_5

not only resulted in loss of lives, but it has exacerbated other global challenges such as famine, equality and socio-economic issues. Additionally, climate change migration is on the rise in different countries. As countries are battling with climate change impacts, they are also concerned with energy poverty impacts including an escalation in deforestation, which is triggered by the continued reliance on traditional energy such as biomass. It has proved hard to have a wholesome energy transition, necessitating scholars to recognise the progressive nature of energy use., which has been termed as Energy Progression.[1] Countries in both the global north and global south are therefore faced with the twin challenge of addressing energy security and climate change while also ensuring that there is a just transition to a low-carbon economy.[2]

This book has therefore analysed the energy transition global landscale as illustrated in Chapter 1. In Chapter 2, the book has discussed the various energy transition risks that policymakers and other stakeholders should be aware of.

The continued reliance on extractives has influenced the discussion in Chapter 3, which analyses the country case studies to ascertain if the extractive contracts align with the net-zero goals. As observed in this chapter, it is worrying that the extractive contracts and the provisions therein, have prima facie not transformed to address climate change or even align with the net-zero goals. The provisions that existed before the signing of the 2015 Paris Agreement, are similar to those in the current contracts signed after 2015. Although there are laws to address environmental and social concerns, policymakers are urged to revise their extractive contracts to ensure that they align with the future net-zero goals and the overall just transition.

While providing the negotiation tools to address the transition risks, Chapter 4 emphasises that the task of renegotiating and implementing net zero and climate-aligned natural resource contracts must start with addressing barriers in existing laws and contracts that may hinder such alignment process. This would require among others, a national strategy and policy that aligns investment frameworks with net zero ambitions.

[1] Nalule V.R., 'How to Respond to Energy Transitions in Africa: Introducing the Energy Progression dialogue' (2021) *Energy Transitions and the Future of the African Energy Sector: Law, Policy and Governance*, 3–5.

[2] Heffron, R.J., *Achieving a Just Transition to a Low-Carbon Economy* (Heidelberg, Germany: Springer, 2021).

5.1 Future Directions

Effectively managing the wide range of transition related risks in the extractive sector will to a large extent depend on specific local circumstances and contexts, and who are the key stakeholders involved in the project (i.e., whether it is a foreign company). The domestic legal frameworks on net zero and the clean energy transition, institutional capacity, supplier development programs and resources for R&D that are available to support just and inclusive outcomes, including transparency in sustainability reporting and disclosures are all key factors that must be carefully considered when designing, planning, and negotiating extractive investment opportunities in a net zero era. Extractive sector investors will need to carefully understand the scope of justice risks that their investments face in a country context, and how to comprehensively anticipate and address such risks through proactive and enterprise-wide risk management frameworks. Anticipatory and effective risk management frameworks should coherently align extractive operations with international treaty norms on climate change, trade, investment, gender, environment, human rights, and sustainable development. Further, and importantly, foreign companies have also to consider their international activities and also those of their home nation, and there are many calls of how they need to adapt their corporate strategies, and this is a key future area of research importance.[3]

Furthermore, as countries and business enterprises worldwide release net zero and clean energy transition plans and programs, lawyers representing companies and investors in negotiating extractive agreements, must emphasize the wisdom in early due diligence to properly evaluate and manage transition-related risks. Even in countries without clear national action plans on business and human rights, or climate change legislation, the increasing emphasis in Europe, North America and other parts of the world on responsible and ESG compliant investments could mean that failure to properly evaluate, price and address justice risks may reduce access to financing, insurance, export competitiveness and overall profitability of extractive investments if operations are deemed not to meet the stringent ESG requirements in foreign markets. Such increased

[3] Heffron, R.J., 'Repurposing for the Just Transition: Energy Companies Need to Future-Proof Their Structure and Strategy' (2023) 16(3) *Journal of World Energy Law and Business*, 302–307.

global emphasis on transparency, ESG, and responsible investment therefore call for a holistic human rights and environmental due diligence that evaluates the ESG regulatory landscape and spots and addresses all risks. Nearly all cases of conflict over incompatibility of net zero programs with contractual obligations in extractive contracts arise from a mismatch of expectations on the scope of transition requirements. There is a strong business case, in terms of cost, reputation and effectiveness, for investors and host countries alike, to clarify the scope of transition related obligations from the early stages of negotiation. As discussed in this book, net-zero aligned contracts can promote greater clarity and certainty on net zero obligations, while also providing clear frameworks for timely and effective dispute resolution.

Similarly, the importance of transparent data collection, benchmarking and monitoring cannot be overemphasized. Several of the disputes and claims relating to greenwashing stem from lack of clear guidelines on how net zero performance data is to be collated, reported and evaluated. There is an urgent role for extractive sector regulators to clarify net zero disclosure requirements and standards that investors should comply with in reporting their net zero programs and performance. Such clarity will not only increase the chances of compliance and effectiveness, it will also go a long way in boosting the investment climate and competitiveness of a country by reducing ambiguities and risks associated with investing in the extractive sector. To maximize such investment and sustainable development outcomes, such net zero disclosure requirements and standards must be flexible, adaptable and constantly monitored and updated in light of best available information and technology. On the other hand, extractive sector investors themselves should invest in technologies and benchmarking tools that enhances transparent collection and reporting of their net zero performance, as well as climate risks and opportunities.

Finally, establishing training and capacity development programs to enhance understanding and awareness on the continuous monitoring of net zero programs and outcomes, in light of overall sustainable development goals and aims, is a crucial requirement for promoting contract transparency and progress on net zero. For example, the Nigerian Content Research and Development Fund (NCR&DF) aims to promote robust research and development (R&D) that will bridge local capacity, technology, and interoperability gaps in the country's extractive sector.[4] Establishing similar R&D innovation programs at country and company levels, can go a long way in improving the capacity of extractive sector workers to understand the complexities of net zero programs. It would also enable such workers to acquire the skillsets needed to meet contractual obligations relating to transparent data collection, reporting and disclosure.

Regional and international knowledge sharing platforms to promote the exchange of resources, clean technologies and information need to advance net zero in the extractive sector will also be key. International cooperation and North–South solidarity on capacity development, training and technology transfer will also need to be prioritized over the next decade in order to provide extractive sector worldwide, especially in Global South countries, with latest technology and tools to effectively advance a just and inclusive clean energy transition. Further research on addressing legal and institutional barriers to the diffusion and absorption of clean energy technologies in extractive sector operations, especially remote sensing technologies needed to better detect, monitor, and measure GHG emissions and progress on net zero, will be fundamental going forward.[5]

Overall, this book highlights issues of risk in one key sector in many economies. There is an issue here that for too long this has gone unaddressed, and climate change, a just transition and net-zero plans have all accelerated the need for this risk to managed more effectively. In this context one growing area of research for all scholars is that it is now time to establish a new social contract for energy sector operations among all stakeholders.[6] This new social contract can be researched in many ways and even the United Nations has launched its own agenda in exploring this.

[4] See Bello, O., 'NCDMB Governing Council Approves $50 m for Research and Development' (July 5, 2020), https://businessday.ng/news/article/ncdmb-governingcouncil-approves-50m-for-research-and-development/, accessed 20 September, 2023.

[5] Babalola, A., and Olawuyi, D., 'Overcoming Regulatory Failure in the Design and Implementation of Gas Flaring Policies: The Potential and Promise of an Energy Justice Approach' (2022) 4(11) *Sustainability*.

[6] Heffron, R.J., and De Fontenelle, L., 'Implementing Energy Justice through a New Social Contract' (2023) 41(2) *Journal of Energy and Natural Resources Law*, 141–155.

Index

V. R. Nalule et al., *Renegotiating Contracts for the Energy Transition in the Extractives Industry*, Just Transitions,
https://doi.org/10.1007/978-3-031-46258-0

Printed in the United States
by Baker & Taylor Publisher Services